HOW TO MAKE MONEY ONLINE USING CHATGPT

QUIT YOUR DAY JOB AND EARN FULL-TIME INCOME USING CHATGPT EVEN IF YOU HAVE ZERO EXPERIENCE (A COMPLETE EASY-TO-UNDERSTAND AND UP-TO-DATE GUIDE FOR BEGINNERS)

ANDREW HARRISSON

CONTENTS

PART FIVE
THE ACTUAL BUSINESS

PART SIX
FREELANCING WITH CHATGPT

PART SEVEN
WHAT'S NEXT?

INTRODUCTION

If you don't innovate fast, disrupt your industry, disrupt yourself, you will be left behind.

JOHN CHAMBERS

Grant worked as a sales representative in a tech company for six years. His duties consisted of selling software products to small business owners, saving them time and money. The year 2020 hit, and his job was one of the first to be cut. Due to COVID-19, his company had to down-size, and they simply didn't need as many sales reps.

That's when Grant realized that relying on a single source of income wasn't enough. At any moment, he could find himself unemployed and stranded. Fortunately for him, he hadn't started a family yet, but what if he had?

Over the next year and a half, Grant survived on freelance virtual assistant jobs found online. He was amazed at how much money he could make staying at home and dedicating at least 10 hours a day to internet tasks. He was surprised to earn twice as much money offering services online than he did at his traditional 9-to-5. Plus, since he was now his own boss, he could generate multiple sources of income, using basic technological tools, and avoid the risk of ending up at rock bottom again.

Many people fear the transition from corporate to entrepreneurship because of the perceived security a 9-to-5 offers. But what happens when the economy crashes or new technological inventions are introduced and the demands for labor change in the workforce? How secure is your office job then?

The truth of the matter is that there is risk in everything nowadays. As Mark Zuckerberg once put it, "The biggest risk is not taking any risk. In a world that's changing really quickly, the only strategy that is guaranteed to fail is not taking risks" (Sylva, 2017). Living off a single source of income is risky, but so is venturing into the world of freelancing or starting your own business. The real question you need to ask yourself is: *What risk would I regret if I didn't take it?*

If you are somebody who follows work trends, you will notice many people who share similar career stories as Grant. They started out working full-time at a company but realized that they weren't maximizing their time and earning potential. They were spending 40 hours per week helping some rich guy or family build their empire, while they lived paycheck-to-paycheck—knowing that they could be fired at any moment. After this sudden realization, they explored part-time or contract jobs on the internet that could supplement their income, or become a side hustle.

Your time is a precious commodity, and sadly you don't have a lot of it. How you choose to spend your time determines how soon you make those seven figures and retire on a private island. The traditional 9-to-5 won't speed up this journey, it will only make it longer—especially if it is your only source of income. Technological advancements have created new ways of making money over the internet, which don't require technical knowledge or years of work experience.

In this particular book, we will explore ways of making money using one of the most controversial technological inventions: artificial intelligence (AI). You have probably heard about AI by now, the sophisticated computer systems that are able to perform cognitive functions like learning language, problem-solving, interpreting patterns, and recognizing speech. If this is starting to sound like a human mind, that's because AI tools are designed to mimic human thinking, even though there are still many years to go before they can replace humans in a work environment.

One specific tool that has everybody talking is an application called Chat-GPT, developed by the company OpenAI. This nifty chatbot functions as a language processing tool that is able to generate solutions and even offer valuable feedback—faster than you can think, too. But this doesn't make ChatGPT an enemy to your career development. In fact, the more you learn and understand how to use this tool, the sooner you can start making money from it!

Think about it: If you are more efficient at carrying out tasks that require a bit of thinking, like brainstorming innovative ideas, writing catchy copy for ads, or gathering curated information about a specific target audience, you can start an online business or take on multiple freelancing jobs, without necessarily giving up more time. The end goal is making more money in less time, and the only thing you need is a stable internet connection.

The aim of this book is to teach you the specific steps and methods on how to integrate ChatGPT into your online business model, including freelancing, to achieve success and make money online. If you haven't read up about AI or ChatGPT before, don't fret! This is a beginner's guide that provides background information on this specific technology and how you can use it to your benefit.

The best part is that you are being mentored by me, a successful tech entrepreneur and programmer, if I may boast. My name is Andrew Harrison, and I am passionate about entrepreneurship and generating wealth.

I have seen firsthand the power of AI in building and growing businesses. Furthermore, I've made it my mission to keep up with the latest trends and research in AI's usage. I'm particularly interested in the rise of ChatGPT and how it can be integrated into business models to increase turnover and facilitate success.

I worked as a programmer for a large corporation before spreading my wings and starting my own business. I was armed with a determination to succeed, and I overcame significant hardships in order to ensure my business indeed succeeded. My commitment and dedication saw me through some challenging times, but I've arrived at a point where I am now financially free. With the full knowledge that financial freedom is possible no matter what hurdles stand in the way, I am now very enthusiastic about helping others experience the same success.

Are you looking for more ways to make money, but aren't ready to say goodbye to your day job? Or are you an entrepreneur looking for the next big tech trend to capitalize on? Either way, this book has been created to help you take the first leap into the world of AI and discover what the craze is about!

PART ONE
THE FUNDAMENTALS

CHAPTER 1
GETTING STARTED WITH CHATGPT

Today's technology was yesterday's science fiction.

RODRIGUE RIZK

WHAT IS CHATGPT?

Y ou may have already witnessed the buzz around the generative AI tool called ChatGPT. Within five days of launch, over 40% of US adults had read up about it (Statista, 2023). This goes to show just how disruptive the invention has been to the tech world. Before we take a look at what ChatGPT is about, it is important to understand the system it is built from—generative AI.

Generative AI is a type of artificial intelligence system that is designed to produce various kinds of content, including text, images, videos, code, and audio. Traditionally, content producers, such as writers, filmmakers, or artists would use their own human intelligence to come up with fresh and relevant content. But with generative AI, machines can be taught how to brainstorm, create, edit, or provide feedback on content.

ChatGPT is a generative AI tool created by a company called OpenAI. The company released the first version of the tool to the general public in November 2022, for testing. Since then, there have been a number of updates made to the tool, and the most recent version, GPT4, was released in March 2023. There is a free and subscription-based plan offered to customers. The paid plan costs $20 per month (as of June 2023) and gives you access to the most recent updates.

The best way to describe ChatGPT is a chatbot that allows you to source and gather information through conversational interactions. Not everybody uses the tool to create content, as some primarily use it for research, clarifying ideas, refining arguments, or planning the structure of essays or other projects. As the chatbot becomes more sophisticated, it is capable of asking follow-up questions, challenging your assumptions, admitting its own mistakes, and turning down inappropriate requests.

HOW CHATGPT WORKS

You may be wondering how exactly this is possible. The creators of ChatGPT trained the machine to think and respond in human-like ways. They fed it large amounts of data sourced from different data portals and hired human AI trainers to ask thousands of questions and facilitate dialogue with the chatbot. Through repetition and fine-tuning, the chatbot was able to think and respond in more predictable ways. For example, when prompted to provide information about a historical event, it would only select relevant information based on the period and the specific context of the question.

ChatGPT is often compared to Google's search engine because both are built on two phases: a data gathering phase and an interaction phase. Before sourcing information from Google or ChatGPT, you must enter a prompt or keywords that allow the system to pull large sums of data. Thereafter, you can interact with the data by adding follow-up prompts or keywords.

However, ChatGPT was not created to be a replacement for Google. The main difference between the chatbot and search engine is that the former was designed to be a supplement to human knowledge; a type of virtual assistant, if you like. The information sourced on ChatGPT is meant to enhance the quality and depth of existing knowledge. With ChatGPT, you are not looking for new information (as you would on a search engine like Google), but you are looking for meaningful answers to improve what you already know and are capable of doing.

For example, ChatGPT wouldn't be an appropriate tool to learn the steps of writing a book. Google's search engine would be the best place to find that kind of information. Instead, ChatGPT could help you find the best ways to structure your essay, plan what type of content to include, and proofread the completed piece for you. Can you see the difference in usage?

IN SUMMARY

- Generative AI is a type of artificial intelligence system that teaches machines how to produce new and relevant content. Newer AI tools, such as ChatGPT, have been built on this particular system.
- The general public first heard about ChatGPT in November 2022. Within the first few days, over 40% of the US adult population knew about the technology.
- ChatGPT can be described as a chatbot that facilitates human-like interactions, as though you were having a conversation with your personal virtual assistant. You are able to ask the chatbot questions and it can pull up relevant data.

Now that you are familiar with what ChatGPT is about, the next chapter will go into greater detail on how to use it effectively.

CHAPTER 2
HOW TO USE CHATGPT

There's a certain feeling that happens when a new technology adjusts your thinking about computing. Google did it. Firefox did it. AWS did it. iPhone did it. OpenAI is doing it with ChatGPT.

AARON LEVIE

HOW TO ACCESS CHATGPT

The best way to learn about the features of ChatGPT is to test it! Below are beginner-friendly instructions on how to access the chatbot:

1. Sign up for a free OpenAI account

Go to https://chat.openai.com/auth/login and click on the "Sign Up" button. Register a new account by providing an email address, or a Google, Microsoft, or Apple account. Afterward, you will be prompted to provide information about yourself, such as your full name, date of birth, and phone number. This data is only used for verification purposes.

2. Familiarize yourself with the ChatGPT interface

After you have successfully registered an account, you will be guided to the ChatGPT dashboard. Before clicking on any tabs or links, familiarize yourself with the layout and various features on display.

3. Start creating prompts or questions

Depending on the model of ChatGPT you are using, you will see the following items on your screen:

- "New Chat" button: Toward the top-left corner of your screen, you will find a sidebar with a button that will help you start a conversation with the chatbot whenever you want. Hit this button whenever you want to begin a new thought without any referral to previous data collected from other prompts.
- Chat history: The sidebar will also include a history of the conversations you have started with the bot, as well as provide the options of editing, deleting, or sharing the link to the chat.
- Account: At the bottom of the sidebar is a button with your name that leads you to account-related information.
- "Send a message" prompt: Starting a "new chat" enables you to enter your questions on what looks like a search bar. Click "enter" and the chatbot will begin gathering curated data.
- ChatGPT responses: Shortly after sending your question, you will see the ChatGPT icon appear at the center of your screen. The bot will then list all of the relevant information it was able to source. Next to the icon, there will be thumbs up, thumbs down, and copy buttons to rate the quality of the response.
- Regenerate response: At the bottom of the page, you will see the "regenerate response" button, which prompts ChatGPT to search through its data archives for more relevant and meaningful data related to your question.

It is important to remember that ChatGPT won't always produce accurate or relevant results. In essence, the machine is only as smart as it has been trained to be. Moreover, the results are based on the data the chatbot is fed, and some questions may require information the machine doesn't have access to.

IS CHATGPT FREE?

ChatGPT is a free tool to use, for the time being. The developers at OpenAI are still in the testing and reviewing phase of the project, which means that they won't charge you to ask prompts and questions.

There is, however, an option to upgrade your free subscription plan to a paid plan called "ChatGPT Plus." This plan will cost you $20 per month and gives you priority access to new features.

CAPABILITIES

The developers at OpenAI are hard at work, bringing new updates to the ChatGPT models. Built on a generative AI system, the possibilities of what ChatGPT can do are endless. However, for now, here are some of the awesome features of the chatbot:

1. Text generation

One of the main elements of ChatGPT is its ability to generate information. This is how it is able to start a conversation with the user. After a prompt is entered, the chatbot will complete a quick search through its database and generate text that is relevant and appropriate to the question asked.

2. Text completion

A unique feature of ChatGPT is the ability to complete sentences with meaningful content. You may be writing a caption for a social media post, but don't have the perfect ending. Or perhaps you want to describe the service offerings for your business but aren't familiar with the right jargon. ChatGPT will attempt to complete your thoughts by providing the best keywords and phrases stored in its database.

3. Summarization

If you don't have the time or desire to read through long research journals, reports, or books, ChatGPT can summarize the information for you. All you need to do is command it to look over a certain number of pages, or certain chapters, and pull up specific information. It may not be able to complete full-length books or report reviews, but condensing the information from a few pages is possible.

4. Text translation

Another useful feature of ChatGPT is its translation tool. Similar to Google Translate, you are able to command the chatbot to translate text from one language into another. Of course, there are limitations. For instance, based on pretrained knowledge, ChatGPT may not be able to translate text into some foreign languages. It could also make a few grammatical or phrasing mistakes and overlook certain details.

5. Sentiment analysis

Even though ChatGPT does not have emotional intelligence, it can detect human sentiments in text, like whether a comment left by a customer is positive or negative. This feature can be useful when conducting market research and seeking to gain unique insights to improve business offerings.

LIMITATIONS

ChatGPT has revolutionized the way we consume and create content. However, it is not without faults. Since the chatbot is trained by human AI developers and relies on preexisting data sourced on the internet, there are some functions that it cannot perform, such as:

1. Lack of human intelligence

There is no doubt that ChatGPT is one of the most advanced AI models created in our time, but it does not replace human reasoning. For instance, the bot can generate contextualized answers but isn't able to understand the meaning of the text. This means that sometimes the responses are generic, incorrect, or don't make any sense. It still relies on a human being to verify its responses and fill in the gaps.

2. Biased or discriminatory responses

Due to the inability to verify its own responses and check for inappropriate language, ChatGPT can sometimes generate answers that are offensive to some users. The bot was trained with a large amount of data from the internet, and some of the input contains biases. Moreover, since the training data is limited (the cutoff year is 2021), new data that represents more modern and current perspectives has not been included.

3. Repetitive outputs

Another limitation of ChatGPT is the use of repetitive text when generating responses for similar, but different questions. This results in generic responses that don't provide in-depth meaning or fresh insights. If you are reading a story created on ChatGPT, it can sound elementary or unimaginative.

4. Plagiarism issues

ChatGPT is incapable of generating unique data. The responses generated by the bot are variations of existing information from multiple
sources on the internet. Thus, if you intend on using the text for academic
submissions or commercial use, it will be flagged high for plagiarism or
copyright infringements. It is best to build upon the text and add your
own creative flare, instead of copying and pasting it in its original form.

5. Availability

Due to the fact that accessing ChatGPT is free, the system can sometimes
crash or become overloaded with users. When this occurs, you will see a
message on your screen that reads: "ChatGPT is at capacity." You may
have to wait a few minutes and refresh your page before gaining access.

IN SUMMARY

- For the time being, accessing ChatGPT is free. All you need to do
  is sign up for an account, take a moment to familiarize yourself
  with the interface, and start sending prompts and questions.
- What makes ChatGPT so impressive are the various features it
  contains, such as the ability to generate text, summarize lengthy
  information, translate text to different languages, and detect the
  sentiment behind words (e.g. whether a review given by a
  customer is positive or negative).
- Since ChatGPT cannot produce unique data, it relies on other
  people's work sourced from the internet. It is therefore your
  responsibility to edit the text and add your own creative spin to
  avoid plagiarism or copyright issues.

Now that you are familiar with how to use ChatGPT, the next chapter
will go into greater detail on the different types of content you can create
using the bot.

CHAPTER 3
A CONTENT CREATOR'S DREAM

It won't be a surprise to see in the next 24 months, multiple billion-dollar companies built on top of OpenAI's foundational models.

DAVID SHIM

CHATGPT FOR PERSONAL USE

A few years ago, none of us could have imagined relying on AI to help us with personal, business, and educational tasks. The idea of a chatbot helping us produce content or come up with meaningful strategies just seemed too futuristic. However, today we have ChatGPT, which offers us all of these options, and more!

Think of ChatGPT as your free virtual assistant. Whatever support you might need for completing projects, sourcing relevant information, or creating compelling content, you can rely on your helpful chatbot. Below are some of the ways ChatGPT can assist you with everyday tasks:

1. Brainstorm a list of ideas

Since ChatGPT consists of a wealth of data, you can ask it to generate lists of ideas to implement for various projects or interests. For example, if you are planning a vacation abroad, you can ask the chatbot to generate an itinerary for you, based on the country you are visiting and the type of tourist attractions they have to offer. You can also ask the chatbot to generate lists for parenting strategies, routines, music and TV recommendations, and so on.

2. Ask for advice

The problem with searching Google for advice is that you need to filter through the information to find reliable opinions. Some sites may offer bogus advice and others may list medical information that is difficult to interpret. The benefit of asking ChatGPT for advice is that it does the searching and filtering for you, and presents the information in a conversation-like style. The only limitation is that the quality of advice is determined by the quality of data stored in the system. Thus, sometimes you may not get the most current perspective.

3. Learn different ways to explain a concept

The difference between your interpretation of reality and ChatGPT's interpretation of reality is that yours is subjective, while the chatbot's interpretation is objective and varied. If you are researching a concept or theory, you can ask the bot to provide you with multiple definitions and perspectives. For instance, you may want to know the different views of right-wing and left-wing politicians on a specific subject. Or you may want the bot to explain the concept of blockchain technology, like you are a five-year-old.

4. Prepare for a job interview

In true virtual assistant style, ChatGPT can help you prepare for upcoming job interviews. There are different ways to approach interview prep. For example, you could ask the chatbot to pull up frequently asked questions about a specific job role, the best ways to answer specific questions in an interview, a list of do's and don'ts during interviews, and so on. Of course, there is no guarantee that the questions and answers ChatGPT pulls up will be asked in your interview, however, they are still useful when making preparations.

5. Generate email templates

Sometimes you might know what you want to say, but don't have the right words to say it. One of ChatGPT's specialties is coming up with generic scripts for personal use, such as email templates. Whether you want to follow up with a coworker, write a thank-you message, or apply for a job, the chatbot can generate the perfect message which requires minimal changes.

Even though ChatGPT is reliable, make sure that you review responses to detect any inaccurate or inappropriate information. Moreover, for any health or financial advice, it is better to consult a doctor or financier, who may be able to assess your specific needs and make expert recommendations.

DIFFERENT INDUSTRIES AND CHATGPT

There are fears that AI tools like ChatGPT will soon replace thousands of jobs. However, technology in general has been replacing manual, systematic jobs for over a decade now. For example, since the integration of automation in the manufacturing sector in the early 2000s, there have been 1.7 million jobs lost worldwide (L, 2023). It is estimated that more jobs will be replaced by smart machines in the coming years. These are just figures specific to the manufacturing industry—can you imagine how many more jobs have been lost in other sectors?

ChatGPT was not created to replace human labor. As mentioned throughout the book, it is better to see the chatbot as a virtual assistant, at most. It still relies on a human user to feed it data, teach it how to think critically, and start conversations that lead to insights and meaningful content.

If anything, the benefit of inventions like ChatGPT is that they can create new jobs, or at least help you save time on research, planning, and producing content. The World Economic Forum has predicted that AI tools will create more than 133 million new jobs in the future, as a result of establishing a machine-operated workforce (Vega, 2019). In other words, jobs that can be done faster and cheaper with a machine, such as administrative and routine work, will be replaced with jobs that cannot be replaced by machines, such as those that require human engagement and emotional intelligence.

With that being said, it is still worth considering the various ways ChatGPT is revolutionizing the workforce, paying close attention to how you can use these changes to your benefit. Below are a few practical applications of ChatGPT in different industries:

Sales and Marketing

Sales and marketing is all about promoting the products or services offered by a business through creating meaningful content. There is a range of sales promotion, content creation, and strategy tasks that ChatGPT can assist with to save time and costs. These might include

- generating sales and marketing copy, including social media captions, and radio and TV scripts.
- generating user manuals and guides, as well as product descriptions.
- analyzing customer feedback data and extracting specific information, such as themes and sentiments.
- improving the efficiency of the sales team by recommending compelling product placement, customer interaction, and revenue growth strategies.

Customer Service

Did you know that you can train ChatGPT to assist with customer support queries using your company data? When integrated into your website, mobile app, WhatsApp messenger, or WordPress blog, the chatbot can act like a human agent and either answer questions or guide customers toward the right channels. Below are some of the customer service applications for ChatGPT:

- improving existing customer chatbots by providing more relevant responses and even creating cross-sell leads
- reading information from product images and detecting errors or defects in order to diagnose the problem and provide meaningful solutions
- handling time-consuming customer support tasks, such as following up with customers by email or addressing FAQs

IT and Programming

ChatGPT isn't going to replace IT jobs any time soon because many of the services and solutions clients are looking for require an advanced level of skill. To compete with human developers, ChatGPT will need to be trained with an enormous amount of data—and many businesses cannot afford to invest that much time and money in AI. Nevertheless, there are various ways ChatGPT can make programming a lot easier. These may include

- generating code and documentation to fast-track projects (an example would be converting basic expressions from one coding language to another).
- automatically completing data tables while adding contextual information.
- generating synthetic data in the absence of real data to improve machine learning.

Risk and Legal

The risk and legal industry comes with a lot of research and administrative tasks, such as reading and analyzing reports, assessing legal documents for errors, formulating contracts, and so on. ChatGPT can assist analysts and legal professionals to complete their jobs with more accuracy and efficiency. Here are some practical applications of ChatGPT in the risk and legal industry:

- generating and review legal documents like contracts, court orders, and patent applications
- reading through and summarizing lengthy legal documents and highlighting discrepancies or issues that need to be addressed
- reading through lengthy legal documents and answering specific questions related to the information

Banking

In the short amount of time that ChatGPT has been around, it has brought about positive changes to the way bankers work. Some of the ways it assists bankers are improving customer service, offering custom financial advice, and performing repetitive tasks. Here are a few more practical applications of ChatGPT in the banking sector:

- generating personalized financial advice and solutions for specific customer personas by training ChatGPT to analyze and draw patterns from in-house customer data
- analyzing fraud data and generating insights that can help bankers protect their customers against fraud and other criminal activity online
- monitoring transaction activities and alerting institutions of suspicious behavior
- automating everyday banking tasks, such as generating emails and reports

REAL-LIFE SUCCESS STORIES

You have read or even heard about the many ways ChatGPT is changing people's lives for the better. Below are real success stories of how the chatbot has helped three people launch lucrative projects!

Writing Books in Hours

Book publishing is one of the most popular ways of earning passive income without investing thousands of dollars into a side hustle. For many self-published authors who want to get books out quickly while saving costs, ChatGPT has become their content tool of choice.

For example, author Brett Schickler wrote a 30-page children's book on ChatGPT within a matter of hours, then proceeded to publish the book on Amazon. After about a week of launching the book, he made $100 in sales. In an interview with Greg Bensinger from Reuters, Schickler shared an example of a prompt he used to generate his story, which was "write a story about a dad teaching his son about financial literacy" (Bensinger, 2023).

After witnessing the success of his debut children's book, Schickler plans on being one of many hundreds of authors who are making careers out of publishing AI-assisted books.

Selling AI-Powered Products

Some entrepreneurs see ChatGPT as an AI tool that could be integrated with other products, like apps or websites, to help them run more efficiently. Furthermore, entrepreneurs who have some knowledge of programming are able to train ChatGPT with their personalized data to assist with niche services.

Self-professed "SEO Nerd," Shawn Hill, created an interactive chatbot using ChatGPT's structure over just a few days. The best part is that he didn't need to do a lot of programming, since the framework had already been built for him. After two days of hard work, Hill sold the chatbot for an impressive $10,000 to the company Originality.AI.

Starting ChatGPT-Operated Businesses

Would you trust ChatGPT to take the position of CEO for your business? Recently, a startup in Portugal did just that, and since launching their T-shirt on-demand business, they predict making an annual profit of over $43,000 (Nucleus AI, 2023).

João F. Santos is the founder of the business *AIsthetic Apparel*, an online store that sells AI-generated T-shirts. He gave himself a challenge to build his startup completely relying on the suggestions given by Chat-GPT, and dedicated an hour a day to executing tasks and advice given by the bot, such as choosing the type of business, creating a compelling business name, and generating a business plan.

Of course, the chatbot completed the bulk of the work, such as providing the business outline and overview, product suggestions, brand images, and descriptions. All that was left for João Santos to do was review the business proposal, set up the online store, seek business partners, and secure funding (ChatGPT helped him source the right investors).

He made an initial investment of $1,000 and secured funding of $2,500 for a 25% share of the company. Within the first week of launching the business, the company made over $10,000 in revenue (about $7,000 net profit).

Are you inspired to come up with your own lucrative project, powered by ChatGPT? If so, keep on reading because the upcoming chapters will show you how!

IN SUMMARY

- There are various personal or professional applications for ChatGPT, which makes this particular AI tool incredibly versatile.
- Whether you are doing research, creating content, seeking advice, or starting a side hustle, ChatGPT can assist you with a range of tasks.
- What's important is being able to identify opportunities for utilizing ChatGPT in your everyday life, such as thinking about how you can save time and money sourcing information and completing repetitive tasks.

Now that you are familiar with the practical applications of ChatGPT, let's cross over to Part 2 and look at ways to make money using the chatbot.

PART TWO
THE "WHYS" AND "WHATS"

CHAPTER 4
WHY MAKE MONEY ONLINE?

Formal education will make you a living; self-education will make you a fortune.

JIM ROHN

GET READY TO MAKE ONLINE FORTUNES

The advent of technology has created more ways to make money than working a traditional 9-to-5 job. The best part is that you don't need to abandon your day job to make an extra income, since many online gigs and businesses don't demand a lot of your time.

If you have ever dreamed of becoming an entrepreneur, now is the best time to flex your business muscles and build your online empire from the ground up. With ready-to-use technologies like ChatGPT, you won't even need to go through the grueling process that many startups have endured. Information is available to you at one click of a button!

You might be partially convinced about the idea of an online business but are held back by certain factors, like your busy work-life schedule or the lack of technical knowledge.

The beauty of having an online business is that you aren't stretched to the max like you would be in the office. Worried about time or skills? Fortunately for you, there are tech tools created to do most of the thinking and execution on your behalf.

Now, if you still need more convincing, here are a few benefits of making money online:

1. You get to control your work life

When you start an online business, you become an entrepreneur. This means that you control what type of tasks you are responsible for, which days and how often you work, and how quickly you scale. If you can only dedicate two hours a day to online tasks, you can structure your business model accordingly.

2. You can work from home

When you run an online business, you don't need to report to an office or pay rent for your brick-and-mortar business. As long as you have a stable internet connection, you can operate the business anywhere in the world, including from the comfort of your home. This also means that you can work at odd hours of the day, or on weekends if you decide. Unlike a store or office building, there aren't any trading hours.

3. You get to set income targets

Unlike a traditional job, where your income is fixed each month, online businesses present you with a blank check. You get to decide what type of business to start, how many projects to take on (if you are a freelancer), and how much you will charge for your products or services. Of course, other factors like sales and marketing will affect your potential income, but the possible revenue streams online are limitless.

4. You create a safety net in case of unemployment

Let's say you are working in an industry that is rapidly changing due to the latest tech innovations. As a result, you are feeling insecure about your future career prospects and fear being replaced by a robot. To mitigate risk, you might decide to start an online business which utilizes the most current technologies, such as AI. This way, even if you are replaced at work, at least you have another source of income to fall back on.

5. You can safely transition into a new career path

The best thing about online businesses is that nobody checks to see what degrees or work experience the company owner has. If you have been thinking about making a career change, starting an online business is the best way to test your new skills and gain experience before making the full transition. Furthermore, since the latest technologies are built with a lot of sophistication, you won't need to know a lot about an industry before jumping straight into it. Just grab some tech tools to assist you along the way!

THE BENEFITS OF MAKING MONEY WITH CHATGPT

You might be thinking "There are hundreds of ways to make money online. Why do it through ChatGPT?"

The answer to this lies in the power of AI technology to help you get tasks done faster, and with greater accuracy! Take a moment and think: Would you prefer coming up with a book idea and outline on your own, or save 8+ hours and ask ChatGPT to help you generate them? I'm sure you would pick the option that saves you time.

What makes generating income through ChatGPT attractive is that you get to save time on tasks that would otherwise demand a lot of brainstorming, research, and execution. Of course, your projects still need to be reviewed and tweaked to ensure they meet your standards, but the upside is that you don't need to sit on your computer the whole day.

Not only is the ChatGPT business model beneficial for entrepreneurs who are juggling several money-making projects, it can also be a great incentive for busy professionals who desperately want to earn additional income, but still need to commit to their 9-to-5 job.

ChatGPT is perfect for startups or freelancers who expect to steadily increase their earnings over time. As the demand for skills and services grows, they are able to deliver projects within a reasonable time, without necessarily hiring additional help. Equipped with their trusted virtual assistant, they can take on more work and earn more money, but keep the time investment to a minimum!

IN SUMMARY

- People often feel the need to choose between traditional and modern ways to make money. The truth is you can embrace both!
- There are many benefits of making money online, but a major one is that you get to control what type of work you do, and how much time to invest in your projects.
- ChatGPT isn't a necessity when completing online tasks, but it can save you a lot of time and money. The AI-powered platform does most of the planning, strategizing, and execution for you, which means that you can scale your business without hiring more help or giving up a lot of time.

Now that you are sold on the idea of making money with ChatGPT, let's cross over to the next chapter and look at various income-generating tasks you can perform on the platform.

CHAPTER 5
EXAMPLES OF INCOME-GENERATING TASKS TO PERFORM ON CHATGPT

When you find an idea that you just can't stop thinking about, that's probably a good one to pursue.

JOSH JAMES

TURNING $100 INTO SIX FIGURES

There are many inspiring stories on the internet about how ambitious individuals challenged themselves to make money using ChatGPT.

One particular guy named Jackson Greathouse Fall, a writer and brand designer by profession, decided that he would challenge himself to turn a $100 capital investment into as much money as possible using the chatbot.

Of course, in the beginning, he didn't know what type of business would generate the most revenue in the shortest time possible. So, guess what he did? He asked ChatGPT to conduct market research and create a viable business strategy for him.

His prompt looked something like this: "You have $100, and your goal is to turn that into as much money as possible in the shortest time possible, without doing anything illegal" (Zinkuka & Mok, 2023). He was committed to performing all of the human labor that ChatGPT instructed him to do. The rest would be done through AI tools and other software available online.

After a few more prompts, a comprehensive business plan was established. The chatbot instructed Jackson to create an online business that offered products and advice to help customers live sustainably. It even helped him come up with the name of the business, which is Green Gadget Guru, and devised a four-step plan on how to launch the company:

1. Purchase domain and hosting for a website (total cost of $15).
2. Create a niche affiliate website (total cost of $45).
3. Take advantage of social media marketing (total cost of $40).
4. Optimize the website for search engines (free of charge using SEO techniques).

Jackson managed to secure funding of a few thousand dollars after the first day of business. According to a tweet, the business is now valued at $25,000. Even though no real products have been sold as of yet, Jackson plans on seeking partnerships with manufacturing companies.

HOW WILL YOU UTILIZE CHATGPT TO MAKE MONEY?

Most of the startup entrepreneurs and freelancers who have made money with ChatGPT took a risk, which ended up paying off. They studied the chatbot features and thought of ways to generate income by making the right prompts.

Do you realize that ChatGPT could be your ticket to online riches? If you are up for the challenge, you can find ways to turn ordinary tasks into money-making projects. Below are examples of flexible and potentially profitable methods of using ChatGPT. These methods can be used for physical or online businesses, and by entrepreneurs or freelancers!

TV, Radio, and Podcast Scripts

If you are looking to be a creative director or producer of a show, you can use ChatGPT to generate scripts or instructions on how to run the show, what each speaker will say, and other visual elements that might add value to the production.

Potential income: $0.10 and $0.50 per word for video scripts.

Copywriting

Copywriting is a broad term that covers different types of short-form text written for sales and marketing purposes. Examples of "copy" include book, website, and product descriptions, as well as sales emails, social media captions, blog articles, and newsletters.

Potential income: $19–$45 per hour for freelance copywriting services.

Book Publishing

Book publishing, as a form of passive income, has been on a steady rise since 2010. Even though print books still dominate the market, there is a growing ebook and audiobook industry. Traditionally, if you were not going to write the book on your own, you would hire a ghostwriter, who normally charges $1–$3 per word, depending on the scope of the project. ChatGPT allows you to save costs on the writing and editing of your manuscript (although you should double-check for errors and plagiarism).

Potential income: $500 per month from one ebook.

Translation Services

Did you know that professional translators are fast becoming the most sought-after freelancers? Part of the reason for this is businesses seeking to expand to new markets and offer multilingual services and products. To save costs, they are able to hire someone who can translate existing documents into different languages. While ChatGPT does translate text, it may not always pick up on subtle cultural nuances. Thus, the best type of documents to translate from one language to another are standard materials like manuals, newsletters, website content, and product descriptions.

Potential income: $36.57 per hour.

Company Branding

Research shows that 4.4 million businesses are launched every year in the US (Commerce Institute, 2023). One way to make money on ChatGPT is to provide a variety of branding services for new businesses, like creating the name and logo, compiling a brand strategy, conducting a competitor analysis, creating a unique selling proposition (USP), and planning social media content.

Potential income: $15–$100+ per hour.

Writing and Fixing Code

If you are in the website design and development space, one of the services you can offer is writing simple codes or fixing website coding issues. For example, you can create simple web tools to customize business websites, or if a client comes to you with a coding problem, ChatGPT can help you find and fix the problem.

Potential income: $15–$30 per hour.

Publishing Online Courses

Did you know that you don't need to be an educator to make money sharing valuable skills and knowledge? ChatGPT takes the hassle out of planning, outlining, and producing scripts and video content for online courses. You can even ask the chatbot to give you ideas on skills that are in demand, and the details of how to structure, price, and advertise your course.

Potential income: $50–$1,000+ per month on an online course.

Writing and Updating Résumés

A résumé is not just a piece of paper. For many job seekers, it is the first (and sometimes last) opportunity to make a good impression. Statistics show professional résumé writing services help 68% of job seekers land a job within 90 days (Radnai, 2023). Writers have the advantage of knowing how to position job candidates in the best light by including the necessary keywords to optimize résumes and create a visually appealing document.

Potential income: $50–$100 for a standard résumé.

Planning Services

It takes the average person around six to eight months to plan an event or trip. Moreover, the more time spent planning, the less likely they are to follow through and take action. You can tap into ChatGPT's wealth of knowledge and help clients plan their next event, vacation, or home remodeling. Based on your prompts, you can come up with detailed lists, budgets, and itineraries to help them save time and commit to their goals.

Potential income: $25–$100 per hour.

Online Customer Support

If you are in the customer services business, ChatGPT can streamline your query, complaint, and feedback processes, which allows you to have a faster response time and continue making customers happy. The chatbot is also useful when you are troubleshooting and seeking advice for unique customer problems. Not only are you able to offer them quicker solutions, but you can also present multiple choices for them to choose from.

Potential income: $15–$20 per hour.

Online Coaching

Online coaching is a multi-billion dollar industry that has benefitted from technologies like AI and modern video-conferencing platforms. ChatGPT can help you build and manage your coaching business by creating quizzes and assessments, designing customized plans for groups and individuals, and finding tips to make your coaching sessions more impactful.

Potential income: $20–$50 per hour.

SEO Services

Search engine optimization (SEO) is a niche service offered by copywriters, which involves searching for specific keywords that rank high on Google search engines and finding skillful ways to include them in copy. Even though this job still requires emotional intelligence and human experience, copywriters can use ChatGPT to conduct a keyword search, generate optimized titles, or link text with third-party websites or businesses.

Potential income: $15–$40 per hour.

IN SUMMARY

- There are many ways to make money using ChatGPT. Depending on your project, you can decide how many tasks to assign to the chatbot.
- Some online projects, specifically those that require human interaction, won't be fully automated. But you can still complete your research and planning using ChatGPT.
- Many people who have made money with ChatGPT took a risk that paid off in the end. If you have an idea for your next stream of income, why not take the risk and streamline your process with ChatGPT?

Now that you are inspired to launch your income-generating project using ChatGPT, let's cross over to the next chapter and look at must-have requirements before getting started.

CHAPTER 6
WHAT ARE THE REQUIREMENTS?

Self discipline is extremely valuable, especially for entrepreneurs. If you lose everything, but you still have self discipline remaining, you'll get back everything you lost and multiple times more.

HENDRITH VANLON SMITH

MAKE THE INITIAL INVESTMENT

One of the barriers that discourages aspiring entrepreneurs from starting their businesses is the lack of capital. Fortunately, online businesses don't require a lot of money upfront, compared to brick-and-mortar businesses.

However, this doesn't mean that your overheads are going to be at zero. You will need to still pay for certain fees and subscriptions, but you may be able to get away with not taking out a loan.

Making money online, even if you are doing it on a freelance basis, means that you will be your own boss. Think about what that would look like for you, given your existing routine. Besides investing capital, how much time and energy will you need to give to your projects?

The sections below will help you start thinking about the initial investment required to build a successful ChatGPT-assisted online business.

TECHNICAL REQUIREMENTS

There are a few preparations you will need to have in place before making money on ChatGPT. Since your operations will be based online, the most important piece of equipment you will need in order to get started is a working laptop or desktop computer. The newer the model, the better, however, it isn't mandatory to have high-tech hardware (unless you are looking to do graphic design). Even pre-owned devices are acceptable, as long as they allow you to complete the range of online tasks you hope to perform.

Due to the fact that ChatGPT is an interactive chatbot, it is crucial to have a stable internet connection. The last thing you want is for your device to freeze or black out as you are receiving information. Plus, when there are a lot of users on the platform, the speed at which the chatbot performs becomes much slower. If you already have an unstable network, the process of waiting and refreshing your screen can be frustrating.

CAPITAL REQUIREMENTS

Ideally, you would have a large sum of cash to cover your startup expenses and help you through the first year of your business. But in reality, not everybody has a pool of money to dip into.

Nevertheless, your online business, no matter how small it may be, will require a certain amount of funds. To determine how much you need, one option is to create a budget and adapt your business model to what you have (recall Jackson Greathouse Fall starting his business with only $100, as described in the previous chapter). Another option is to create a business concept and, through research, determine how much you need.

If you have limited funds to work with, the first option may be viable for you, since it sets a restriction and forces you to be more resourceful with how you spend the budget. ChatGPT can also hold you accountable for how you send money, as long as you indicate your budget in your prompt and follow the instructions given.

LEGAL REQUIREMENTS

Every business that operates as a distinct entity needs to have a legal structure that determines what type of entity it is, how much liability protection the owners have, and what kind of tax benefits they qualify for.

This isn't mandatory if you conduct your business under your legal name. In this case, the type of entity you would form is a sole proprietorship. To conduct business, you would need to use your social security number and legal name. You would also still be expected to obtain the necessary licenses and meet tax requirements.

Instead of starting a business, you may decide to do freelancing. But technically speaking, the law still regards freelancing as a type of business. Since you are exchanging skills or labor for money, and generating an income, you will be classified as a sole proprietor and file taxes like normal business owners.

SKILLSET REQUIREMENTS

There are three crucial skills you need in order to sustain your online business, and two of them are soft skills.

The first is self-discipline, which refers to the ability to follow through with your plans. The reason why you need this skill is because starting a business isn't easy and there will be moments when you feel like giving up. Some challenges may set you back financially or chip away at your confidence, yet the only way to win is to keep moving forward!

The second soft skill is self-management, which can be described as the ability to manage your time and keep up with the demands of your life. Outside of your online business, you have other responsibilities, such as family, health, hobbies, and possibly a day job. Knowing how to prioritize tasks and allocate enough time for every commitment requires good self-management.

Fortunately, there are many free apps and tools online that can help you with scheduling, creating routines, and enhancing your focus. Another free tip to improve self-management is to create a designated workspace at home.

It is true that you can access ChatGPT anywhere and anytime. However, creating a designated workspace can improve your level of focus and discipline. Every time you enter that particular space, your mindset shifts into work mode and you are able to maintain high performance for however many hours you are there.

When choosing a designated workspace, avoid areas of your home that already serve a specific purpose. For instance, your bedroom is where you sleep, not where you complete business tasks. Look for neutral or multipurpose areas of your home to set up your workspace.

The final skill you will need, which is specific to navigating ChatGPT, is prompt writing skills. The quality of your prompts determines the quality of your results. Therefore, even though ChatGPT creates an equal playing field, users who know how to generate skillful prompts often unlock more opportunities on the platform.

IN SUMMARY

- To get started on making money with ChatGPT, you will need to have a working laptop or desktop computer, a stable internet connection, and a designated workspace. If you have met these requirements, you have the minimum tools to build a successful online business.

- Of course, you will want to get the most out of your experience, and the best way to do that is to have the required capital to build a quality product or offer competitive services.
- Whether you are going the freelancing or entrepreneurial route, you will also need to think about the legal aspects of operating an online business, such as registering your company and filing taxes.

Now that you are familiar with the requirements, let's cross over to Part 3 and look at ways to use ChatGPT effectively.

PART THREE
OPTIMIZING PRODUCTIVITY WITH CHATGPT

CHAPTER 7
THE POWER OF CHATGPT PROMPTS

It takes intelligence to recognize intelligence, or the lack of it.

ARNE KLINGENBERG

WHAT IS PROMPT ENGINEERING?

An important skill you need to learn and understand when using AI chatbots like ChatGPT is prompting. Essentially, this is the only form of communication you will have with the chatbot. Think of it as the AI language that ChatGPT responds to. When you know how to prompt effectively, the chatbot can deliver optimal responses.

Prompt engineering refers to telling an AI chatbot exactly what you want it to do. This is usually done through instructions, and sometimes examples of the type of information you need. If you don't have an example to provide, you can describe what you are searching for to the best of your ability.

Effective prompt engineering is about translating your elaborate ideas or requests into simple and concise language. Since you are speaking to an AI chatbot and not a real human being, you cannot leave room for assumptions. ChatGPT cannot read between the lines or intuitively understand what you want. It can only follow the prompt you have provided and get answers that come close to what you want.

The main purpose of prompt engineering is to maximize the efficiency of the chatbot, getting the most out of it. The fact is that even though ChatGPT is trained using a wealth of data, it is only as "smart" as you program it to be. The only way you will be able to see the true performance and usefulness of the chatbot is to learn how to speak its language!

For example, if you were asking a human friend to provide a summary of the book they are reading, you would probably say "Tell me about the book." Since they know what you are referring to and the expectation you have, they will respond by giving you the book summary.

But ChatGPT requires you to elaborate on what you need, leaving no room for guessing. Preferably, it wants you to explain the request as though you were speaking to a fifth grader. Thus, instead of prompting with "Tell me about the book," you would say "Please provide a summary of the book, mentioning the plot, main characters, and themes explored, in less than 500 words."

Do you notice the difference between the two prompts? The second one is specific and takes into consideration every piece of information the chatbot may need in order to pull the best results. It also doesn't make assumptions, such as thinking the chatbot knows that a book summary includes a discussion of the plot and main themes and characters. With this detailed request, the chatbot will be able to deliver a more accurate response.

The Importance of Prompt Engineering

Did you know that prompt engineering is becoming a highly sought-after skill after the launch of ChatGPT? Those who have mastered prompting are able to save businesses thousands of dollars, which makes them an asset to any organization.

This skill is important because it helps you mine value out of ChatGPT, something that the chatbot cannot do for you. The data is ready and accessible, but your prompts determine how much you can extract.

Of course, not everybody wants to use ChatGPT to build and scale businesses. As a result, learning how to prompt isn't that big of a deal. However, budding entrepreneurs who intend on using ChatGPT as a business tool must be able to engineer prompts.

Since this skill is in high demand, you may even find opportunities to offer prompt engineering services. That's right! Your job could be to help individuals and companies save time and money by getting the most out of ChatGPT. Many clients would need to see proof that you have mastered the skill, such as seeing records of how much money you have made or opportunities you have accessed through ChatGPT.

Believe it or not, this is a booming industry in its own right, and companies across the world are looking for the best prompt engineers. Examples of the type of jobs that are listed online include the following:

- Generative AI trainer (part-time)
- Prompt engineer (part-time)
- Generative AI content creator
- AI visual artist
- AI psychologist
- ChatGPT project manager
- AI character developer
- AI prompt generator
- ChatGPT consultant

Prompt engineers can make between $30–$50 per hour, depending on their level of skill and experience. However, some companies may expect you to have studied a course or completed a degree in computer science, software engineering, or any other related field.

Limitations of AI Prompting

Businessman Robert LoCascio is the founder of EqualAI, a nonprofit organization committed to reducing unconscious bias in the use and development of AI. He recently wrote an article for Fast Company pointing out the limitations of prompt engineering.

This all started with a specific prompt provided to the chatbot: "Write a 750-1 word article about how AI is becoming the 'digital front door' for brands, and make it seem like a Fast Company article" (LoCascio, 2023). It was no surprise that ChatGPT was capable of producing a quality content piece, mentioning all of the main benefits of AI for brands, such as personalized marketing, better research and reporting, and cutting costs.

However, the elephant in the room was that the article sounded manufactured, rather than authentic. According to LaCascio, it lacked creativity and unique insights that a thought leader article would normally have. While the prompt was able to pull up the facts, the writing didn't feel human.

From a business perspective, consider how quality but generic information would impact your ability to make complex decisions, like how to enhance customer experience without doing what every other business is doing. The challenge that ChatGPT is still seeking to solve is going beyond facts and extracting unique insights, or creating content that has never been created before.

Until then, you may experience challenges when engineering prompts on the chatbot, one of them being misunderstanding the intended meaning. When creating prompts, you may run into a situation where the chatbot misunderstands certain phrases due to the lack of contextual information or biases. If you use slang or words only known within a specific culture, you may also run into incorrect information.

Since ChatGPT lacks emotional intelligence, it may not always be helpful when it comes to making value judgments or being sensitive to ethical concerns. Some of the training data may consist of biases or stereotypes, which don't take into consideration new and unique socioeconomic and political contexts.

TYPES OF PROMPTS

There are different ways to structure prompts in order to get the best responses. Depending on what kind of information you are looking for, your prompts can be straightforward or layered. Note that "layered" doesn't mean complicated or confusing, since this will defeat the purpose. Layered prompts are simple but consist of many parts. The quality and clarity of your prompts is the same whether you are crafting a short or lengthy sentence.

Here are three types of prompts and examples to show you how to use them:

Zero-Shot Prompting

Zero-shot prompting is an open-ended type of prompt that leaves most of the legwork to the chatbot. Instead of being specific about what you are looking for, you allow the bot to search through its data, attempt to interpret what you meant, and respond with the best response. In most cases, you will notice that the chatbot offers more than one possible answer (e.g. giving you five strategies rather than one) to ensure you find what you are looking for.

Example prompt:

Create a schedule for a typical productive morning (without descriptions).

ChatGPT results (OpenAI, 2023):

Here's a schedule for a typical productive morning:
6:00 am - Wake up
6:15 am - Exercise
7:00 am - Shower and get ready for the day
7:30 am - Eat a healthy breakfast
8:00 am - Plan and prioritize tasks for the day
8:15 am - Check and respond to emails
8:30 am - Focus on the most important task
9:30 am - Take a short break and stretch
9:45 am - Continue working on tasks or attend meetings
10:30 am - Review progress and make adjustments if necessary
Remember, this is just a general schedule and can be adjusted according to personal preferences and specific circumstances.

One-Shot Prompting

Prompts get a little bit more specific when you are using the one-shot prompting method. To guide the data mining and collection phases, you create a simple description of what you are looking for and one example to make the instruction easier to understand. ChatGPT will take the short description and example and look through its database for information with similar patterns. You are less likely to get multiple options when using this type of prompt because your request filters through a lot of information.

Example prompt:

Create a two-minute, daily workout routine that can help me lose

5 pounds (2 kilograms) per month. Example: 10 reps sit-ups. Keep descriptions short.

ChatGPT results (OpenAI, 2023):

> Here's a simple two-minute daily workout routine that can help you lose 5 pounds (2 kilograms) per month:
>
> 1. Jumping jacks (30 seconds)
> 2. Push-ups (10 reps)
> 3. Squats (10 reps)
> 4. Mountain climbers (30 seconds)
> 5. Lunges (10 reps each leg)
> 6. Plank (30 seconds)
> 7. Bicycle crunches (10 reps each side)
> 8. High knees (30 seconds)
> 9. Tricep dips (10 reps)
> 10. Burpees (10 reps)

Perform each exercise with proper form and take minimal rest between exercises. Increase the intensity and repetitions as you progress. Remember to combine this workout routine with a balanced diet and healthy lifestyle choices for effective weight loss.

Few-Shot Prompting

If you are looking for very detailed and accurate responses that allow minimal room for error, you can use few-shot prompting. Similar to one-shot prompting, you create a description of what you are looking for, but instead of providing one example, you give between 2–10 examples. The examples enable the chatbot to learn a new thought pattern so that the responses match the framework you have given. Note that you aren't retraining the chatbot—rather, you are guiding it on how to gather, interpret, and present information for your particular request.

Example prompt:

> A true friend...
> Example: Gossips behind your back - False
> Example: Offers emotional support - True
> Example: Does not apologize after offending you - False
> Example: Respects your boundaries - True
> Classify this statement: Downplays your success

ChatGPT results (OpenAI, 2023):

> Classify this statement: False.
> A true friend does not downplay your success. Instead, they celebrate your achievements and support you in your accomplishments.

You might be wondering which types of prompts are better to use. The answer is it depends on what you are looking for, and the best way to communicate your ideas. Sometimes, you may not be looking for a specific response and can therefore leave most of the work to the chatbot. But if you need 100% accuracy, or for the chatbot to complete a pattern you have already begun, then you may need to add a lot of detail to your prompts.

TIPS TO OPTIMIZE YOUR PROMPTS

When creating prompts, you always run the risk of being vague, too wordy, or contradictory in what you are searching for. In most cases, this happens because you forget that you are interacting with an AI tool, rather than a human being who has similar thought processes.

Knowing how to optimize your prompts can reduce inconsistencies, save you time, and ensure you pull relevant information. Here are some tips to help you generate effective prompts:

- **Figure out what you want to achieve.** If you start with a goal in mind, you are able to explain what you are looking for with greater clarity. Plus, you will have an indication of how much detail to include in your prompt.
- **Determine how you will measure results.** Along with setting a goal, it is important to determine how you will know when you have received the desired answer. For example, are you looking for a statistic, percentage, strategy, or step-by-step process? In your prompt, ensure that you include a metric to achieve accuracy.
- **A/B testing.** Since ChatGPT isn't 100% accurate, it is recommended that you conduct A/B, or split testing, where you ask the same prompt in two different ways to find out which one generates the best results.
- **Use punctuation and spacing to clarify your instructions.** To convert human language into AI language, your prompt needs to be well-structured. Inserting punctuation and spacing can help you separate two ideas or thoughts, or make a distinction between your prompt and each example provided. Examples of punctuation to use are quotation marks, colons, hashtags, commas, and periods.
- **Don't shy away from examples.** The better you are at explaining what you need, the higher the quality of your results. Even if you don't know what you are looking for, adding an example of a possible response can make ChatGPT's job easier. Perhaps you are looking for information that follows a specific format, focuses on a particular time frame, or follows a certain kind of pattern. Your examples don't need to be complicated to be useful.

These tips are great, but the only way to improve is to practice generating prompts. Don't worry, making mistakes is part of the process of developing your prompt engineering skills. Make time to play around with ChatGPT and practice creating the three types of prompts mentioned above. Thereafter, you can start thinking about how to make your prompts more detailed and targeted for specific outcomes.

IN SUMMARY

- Prompt engineering allows you to communicate with ChatGPT in a language that it can easily understand. It involves drafting clear and simple sentences to generate the desired responses from the chatbot.
- There are three types of prompts that you can use to generate high-quality results on ChatGPT: zero-shot prompting, one-shot prompting, and few-shot prompting. The prompts range in complexity and allow you to make your request as detailed as you want.
- Some of the ways to optimize your prompts include having a goal in mind, conducting A/B testing to see which prompt is more effective, and adding examples so the chatbot knows what type of information you are looking for.

Now that you understand how to create prompts on ChatGPT, let's cross over to the next chapter and look at ways to use ChatGPT to enhance your productivity.

CHAPTER 8
PRODUCTIVITY HACKS WITH CHATGPT

If you spend too much time thinking about a thing, you'll never get it done.

BRUCE LEE

CAN YOU BE PRODUCTIVE WITH CHATGPT?

Time is the most scarce commodity on the planet. With the increasing tasks and responsibilities you manage on a daily basis, 24 hours a day is just not enough. Ridding yourself of the workload may not be a viable solution, especially if taking on more work is part of your plan to build a successful career, and hopefully take an early retirement.

So, what can you do? Well, turn to ChatGPT, of course!

In the previous chapters, we discussed ways to make money with Chat-GPT. However, it is time to take a break from money chats and focus on how you can create more structure in your day so that you are able to juggle multiple roles and responsibilities without burning out.

ChatGPT is the best-kept secret when it comes to boosting your productivity. As a virtual assistant, the chatbot can share some of your workload and help you complete tasks faster.

A recent study showed that when using ChatGPT, business professionals were able to write various documents faster, and with more accuracy, than when they were performing the task manually. When calculated over an eight-hour work day, the professionals who had AI support showed a productivity increase of 59% (Nielsen, 2023).

The findings also shattered the myth that working faster leads to unnecessary mistakes and lower-quality outcomes. Third-party evaluators were brought in to grade the quality of the documents on a scale of 1–7.

They were not told which documents were written manually or with the assistance of ChatGPT. The scores revealed that business professionals who had AI support performed better overall, receiving an average of 4.5 out of 7, compared to the rest, who received an average of 3.8 out of 7 (Nielsen, 2023).

This study proves that technology doesn't make you lazy, but rather highly productive. The benefit of collaborating with ChatGPT is that you can teach it how to carry out certain tasks, and watch as it performs them better than you could manually!

THREE CORE PRODUCTIVITY PRINCIPLES TO CLAIM BACK YOUR TIME

ChatGPT is great for improving productivity, but it isn't a miracle cure. In other words, if you are currently missing deadlines and playing catch-up with work, you would need to first consider where most of your time is being spent and how to manage it more effectively.

Below are three productivity principles that can help you add structure to your day and prioritize tasks. When you have mastered them, you will be able to zero in on what is important and remove time-wasters, giving you an extra hour or two to spend on meaningful side projects.

Practice the 80/20 Rule

The 80/20 rule is a productivity principle that suggests 20% of your daily tasks bring 80% of value. For instance, if you had a list of 10 tasks to perform in a day, only 2 of them would bring the highest returns.

The reason why this rule is important to understand and practice is due to the fact that you may be living a busy lifestyle, and take on multiple roles as a parent, spouse, employee, and freelancer. Each role comes with its own list of tasks that are disguised as "top priorities." However, the more you analyze these tasks, the more you discover that they fall under the 80% and not the 20%.

It isn't that 80% of tasks are not important, they are just not urgent enough that you need to do them right now. For example, you could postpone them without suffering major consequences. The same cannot be said about tasks that fall under the 20% category. If they are not completed urgently, you will experience immediate consequences, such as missing deadlines, slowing down your progress, and going off-track from achieving your goals.

If you are confused about which tasks fall under the 20% and which don't, make a list of regular tasks for each responsibility you take on, and assign them under one of the following categories:

- **Urgent and important:** Tasks that are emergencies, pressing issues, or deadline-based.
- **Not urgent but important:** Tasks that require focus, planning, and enough time for preparation.
- **Urgent but not important:** Tasks that are distractions, exciting but carry little value, and cause interruptions to your day.
- **Not urgent and not important:** Tasks that are complete time wasters and promote unproductive habits, like overthinking, perfectionism, or procrastination.

Tasks that fall under the categories "Urgent and important" and "Not urgent but important" make up the 20%.

Manage the Inflow of Work

Being busy is not the same as being productive. It is possible to be busy with unimportant tasks that steal precious time away from really urgent matters. Moreover, busyness can sometimes be a cover-up for a lack of boundaries when it comes to accepting and declining tasks and projects.

Since you are limited to only 24 hours in a day, there are certain tasks that you may not be able to complete. For example, after performing the 20% priority tasks, you might only be able to get through three of the 80% tasks. The tasks that you are unable to complete are carried over to the next day, week, or month. This entire process is known as managing the inflow of work.

When work is placed on your desk, what happens next? Do you stop whatever you are working on and pick up the task? Do you hide the work under piles of incomplete work and pray your boss forgets about it? Having a plan for times like these can ensure you are not set back every time a new responsibility is given to you.

The best way to manage the inflow of work is to set up boundaries that offer you more control of your schedule. The most effective boundary you can establish is being able to politely say no. This may sound like:

- "Thank you for the invite but I am unable to attend the event."
- "Thank you for approaching me about this project, but I already have a lot going on."
- "I would be happy to assist you, however, right now I am busy working on something else."

Another way to manage the inflow of work, particularly if you are an entrepreneur who tends to have plenty of business ideas flowing through your mind, is to carry a pocket notebook wherever you go and write down thoughts that jump into your head. Not only can this reduce over-thinking, but it can also help you sit on an idea and look over it, before deciding to take action. In other words, you delay giving yourself more work by simply writing ideas down and promising to get back to them later.

Create Systems

The third productivity principle is to identify repetitive tasks and create systems to get them done. What's great about these types of tasks is that they don't require human effort. They can be automated and still produce quality outcomes.

Creating a system is about breaking down a task into components and finding ways to automate each stage or phase, or at least aspects of the task. Nowadays, you can find software that offer turnkey solutions, such as handling your bookkeeping and accounting, managing customer support, or taking care of marketing and advertising needs.

We also cannot forget to mention AI tools like ChatGPT that can help you plan and execute systems for organizing and performing repetitive tasks. In the end, you are able to save time in one area and reinvest time in another area. You may even have some free time to rest and recharge, since "doing nothing" is also key to maintaining high productivity.

PRODUCTIVITY HACKS WITH CHATGPT

When you have reclaimed your time and can finally manage daily tasks without feeling overburdened, ChatGPT can increase your levels of productivity, allowing you to optimize processes, elevate your skills and knowledge, and achieve goals faster.

Below are clever ways ChatGPT improves your productivity:

- **Generate summaries:** When you don't have time to read long articles, reports, or books, ChatGPT can generate a summary of the content for you, highlighting key points and themes.
- **Research assistance:** Sometimes you know what you are looking for, but don't exactly know how to find it on search engines like Google. The chatbot can assist you with collecting and extracting insights from relevant data.
- **Managing emails:** There are various email tasks that ChatGPT can assist you with, such as drafting emails, creating templates, and scheduling meetings.
- **Proofreading:** If part of your job involves writing documents and other content pieces, you can use the chatbot to proofread your work. Of course, since ChatGPT doesn't offer 100% accuracy, you may need to review the results to make sure no errors were missed.
- **Social media management:** Whether it is a personal or professional account, ChatGPT can help you build and manage your social media. Some of the tasks it is capable of performing include tracking and analyzing social media ads, drafting strategies, and producing and optimizing content.
- **Personal development:** You are never alone on your personal development journey when you have ChatGPT. Not only can the chatbot offer advice, but it can also help you set goals, draft routines and schedules, create to-do lists, help you track your progress, and show you hacks for staying motivated.
- **Legal support:** When you need legal assistance, such as seeking advice, drafting contracts, or researching specific laws, ChatGPT can be a great place to start. Of course, it is not recommended to completely rely on the chatbot for legal advice, as the information may not be accurate or relevant to your current situation.
- **Financial planning:** The best place to start when creating budgets, financial plans, or weighing your investment options is ChatGPT. The chatbot is useful for creating weekly or monthly plans, calculating savings over time, or tracking your expenses.

Once again, for expert financial advice, it is recommended to consult with a banker.

- **Networking:** If you are not somebody who tends to go out and meet people, ChatGPT can bring them to you! By generating specific prompts, the chatbot can identify potential mentors and investors, provide a list of upcoming networking events, and offer tips on how to make the best first impression.

- **Career development:** Take ChatGPT along on your career level-up journey! Some of the ways the chatbot can support you include drafting a career development plan, identifying a skills gap, researching the best courses or qualifications, optimizing your résumé, and creating questions and answers for job interviews.

LIST OF PROMPTS TO GET YOU STARTED

You may not be fully convinced that anAI chatbot can increase your productivity. Well, the only way to find out is to put it to the test!

Below are different kinds of productivity prompts you can use (or customize) to get the best out of ChatGPT:

Prompts for Time Management

Prompt: "Create a schedule for a productive eight-hour work day, as a [occupation]."

Example: Create a schedule for a productive eight-hour work day, as a graphic designer.

Prompt: "Agenda for the meeting is: [Give a summary of the meeting agenda]. Duration of the meeting is [Give a summary of total minutes allocated for the meeting]. Provide a minute-by-minute breakdown of what to speak about."

Example: Agenda for the meeting is: Discussing upcoming team-building event. Duration of the meeting is 15 minutes. Provide a minute-by-minute breakdown of what to speak about.

Prompt: How many minutes/hours should I allocate for [Write down a single task or multiple tasks separated by commas]?

Example: How many minutes/hours should I allocate for reading a 60-page report?

Prompt: My deadline is in [number of days remaining] days' time. I still have [percentage of work incomplete] of work to do. How many minutes/hours should I allocate for completing related tasks each day?

Example: My deadline is in five days. I still have 60% of work to do. How many minutes/hours should I allocate for completing related tasks each day?

Prompts for Task Management

Prompt: "Draft an email to my [relation to the other person] about [summary of topic, request, or issue]."

Example: Draft an email to my sister about traveling to visit her in America this December.

Prompt: "Problem: [explain problem using simple language and sentences]. Provide at least five possible reasons why it is doing this and five possible solutions."

Example: Problem: The website shows an error whenever I click on a new page. Provide at least five possible reasons why it is doing this and five possible solutions.

Prompt: "Proofread the following text: [insert text here]. Identify a list of errors. For example, 'In the second sentence, there is a spelling mistake.'"

Example: Proofread the following text: "My name is Katie. I am twenny eigt. I live on my parent's house." Identify a list of errors. For example "In the second sentence, there is a spelling mistake."

Prompt: "Summarize the key concepts in the book: [Provide book title and author name]."

Example: Summarize the key concepts in the book: Rich Dad Poor Dad by Robert Kiyosaki

Prompt: "Provide constructive feedback on the following caption: [insert social media caption]."

Example: Provide constructive feedback on the following caption: "Treat your father to a hot coffee, on us, this Father's Day. Limited time offer."

Prompt: "Here is my list of tasks today: [insert list of tasks in no particular order]. Help me prioritize them using the Eisenhower Matrix."

Example: Here are my list of tasks today:

1. Meet with my boss for a feedback session.
2. Call the dentist to book an appointment.
3. Attend a brainstorming session with the team.
4. Address customer complaints.
5. Visit the warehouse to check whether new stock has arrived.

Help me prioritize them using the Eisenhower Matrix.

Prompts for Overcoming Procrastination

Prompt: "My main goal for the week is: [state goal using simple language and sentences]. Help me break down the goal into smaller tasks, maximum two tasks per day."

Example: My main goal for the week is: To get my online blog up and running. Help me break down the goal into smaller tasks, maximum two tasks per day.

Prompt: "Help me create a technology detox plan to reduce distractions during normal work hours. For example, I work [write down your work hours]. My main distractions are [list main distractions separated by commas]."

Example: Help me create a technology detox plan to reduce distractions during normal work hours. For example, I work nine hours. My main distractions are Instagram, email notifications, Whatsapp notifications.

Prompt: "Create a 30-day journaling plan, with one prompt each day, to help me [write down a specific area that you would like to journal about for the next 30 days]."

Example: Create a 30-day journaling plan, with one prompt each day, to help me increase motivation about my goals.

Prompt: "Identify five successful women in the [choose a specific field], and provide lessons that I can learn from each individual to help me advance in my career."

Example: Identify five successful women in the finance and banking industry, and provide lessons that I can learn from each individual to help me advance in my career.

IN SUMMARY

- Productivity is about making the most of the 24 hours you have every day. To become productive it is important to assess how you are currently spending your time, and whether those tasks bring the most value.
- ChatGPT can help you step up your productivity levels, but it isn't a miracle cure. To get the most out of the chatbot, you will need to first categorize tasks as high and low priority, manage the inflow of work, and set up systems for repetitive tasks.
- There are hundreds of productivity prompts that can help you manage time effectively, automate repetitive tasks, and maintain motivation as you work toward accomplishing your goals. A few of them have been provided in this chapter, but you are welcome to get creative and draft your own!

Now that you know how to maximize productivity with ChatGPT, let's cross over to Part 4 and look at strategies to build an AI-assisted online business.

PART FOUR
PLANNING YOUR BUSINESS

CHAPTER 9
DEFINING YOUR NICHE

If everybody is doing it one way, there's a good chance you can find your niche by going exactly in the opposite direction.

SAM WALTON

WHAT IS A NICHE MARKET?

When building a business, the tendency for many entrepreneurs is to follow the trend. For instance, if consumers are really into branded stationery, they might open a business selling branded stationery.

What they don't realize is that hundreds of similar businesses will pop up in the next few weeks or months, looking to grab a piece of the pie. In the end, the market for branded stationery would become so saturated that many entrepreneurs would go out of business.

Instead of going with the crowd, and having to share the pie with hundreds of hungry businesses, you can explore emerging markets that aren't necessarily popular but show steady growth throughout the next few years. We call these emerging markets "niche markets."

The word niche describes a product or service that is unique and appeals to a smaller audience. Most likely, the products or services appeal to members of a particular demographic, such as people who live in a geographical location, have certain hobbies and interests, or work in a specific occupation.

A niche market refers to a set of businesses that offer specific products and services that only a certain number of consumers would be attracted to. The offering is so specialized that if you are a customer who doesn't have the specific needs or problems those businesses are offering to solve, you won't find anything interesting about the business.

The advantage that niche businesses have over those that offer general products and services is that they get to save money by offering limited products and services, which also allows them to work faster and become experts or leaders in a small playing field.

For example, Walmart is your everyday convenience store that sells everything under the sun. But being a "jack-of-all-trades" means they are bound to sell some products that they are not known for being the best at selling. If you enjoy freshly brewed coffee made with the finest coffee beans, Walmart isn't the first brand you think of. You are more likely going to think about a niche business that is known for selling quality coffee products and beverages. This doesn't mean Walmart coffee is bad, it's just not something they specialize in.

Having a niche business allows you to focus your resources on a few processes, and have more time and money to spend on marketing and keeping customers happy. As a startup business, you are also able to manage your expenses and remain competitive, without spending a fortune on creating a catalog of products or services.

HOW TO FIND A NICHE MARKET

When finding a niche market, practice thinking small. For example, instead of starting a turnkey publishing company, you can build a business around a specific service that authors need, such as book writing and editing or book marketing. Or if you are thinking about launching an online store, you can sell a single customizable product, rather than a range of products.

Thinking small helps you find gaps in the market that competitors may not be taking advantage of. This is what gives your business an edge, causing it to stand out from the rest. The following tips can also be helpful when conducting market research:

1. Consider your passions and interests

This may not sound like the typical business advice you hear. However, it can be useful when brainstorming niche businesses. Since your offerings are going to be specific to the needs of a small audience, why not imagine yourself as the first customer?

Think about the type of gadgets, activities, or experiences that make you happy. Are you somebody who enjoys reading, collecting vintage items, or maintaining an active lifestyle? What are your hobbies at the moment? As the ideas come into your head, write them down on a piece of paper.

Some of the ideas won't make viable businesses, but others may reveal untapped opportunities in the market. Entertain the thought of turning one of your passions into a business and try to visualize the business model, such as what type of business you would run, what you would sell, and who your customers would be.

2. Be others-minded

Another great tip is to forget about your ambitions of starting a business and focus on real-life needs and issues consumers are experiencing. Give yourself a few weeks or months to research consumer trends and behaviors in various industries. Read the latest reports that you can find, compiled by reputable organizations, and try to understand the challenges consumers are dealing with.

If a statistic or insight strikes a chord with you at any time during the research, write it down. That strong urge to take action is a positive sign that you are interested in responding to that particular need. You might also want to close your eyes and put yourself in the consumer's shoes. Imagine their day-to-day life having to live with that specific inconvenience. If you were in their place, what type of product or service would help you solve the problem?

3. Assess profitability

When you have some ideas of possible niche businesses, the next step is to determine whether your ideas could be turned into a profitable company. At this stage, you are required to use logic, not sentimental feelings, to find out if your ideas can generate revenue.

Bring out your calculator and market research, and look over a few important factors, such as:

- **Product:** How much will it cost to manufacture your product? What type of materials will you need to make your products? Where will they be manufactured and stored?
- **Price:** Are you selling a premium or moderately priced product or service? What key factors determine your price point? How much are competitors charging for similar products or services? How is your price competitive?
- **Customers:** Who would you say is part of your target audience? What are their interests and hobbies? How much disposable income do they have? What type of products or services do they typically purchase (i.e. eco-friendly or handmade)?
- **Location:** Where will your business be based? What expenses will you need to factor in when pricing your goods (i.e.

transaction fees for online stories)? How easily will customers find your business?

- **Marketing:** How do you plan on promoting your products or services? How much will it cost to brand and package your goods? How much will it cost to advertise your goods?

These tips are supposed to aid in the search for your niche business. Although, if you don't have a lot of time to spend searching the internet, then you may want to call upon the support of ChatGPT and let the chatbot do most of the brainstorming, researching, and market analysis for you!

DISCOVERING YOUR NICHE USING CHATGPT

Even though ChatGPT cannot predict the future, it is a highly intelligent tool that can synthesize and draw patterns from large data to help you come up with a niche business idea.

However, don't be fooled. It takes a lot more than typing "Generate a list of niche business ideas" to maximize the full potential of the chatbot. You will need to systematically use different prompts to draw a large pool of information, which can reveal untapped opportunities and give you a competitive advantage.

One of the ways to do this is by searching for high-volume keywords using ChatGPT. This can help you verify whether there is a market for your niche business ideas. These keywords will show you what kinds of related topics consumers mostly search for on sites like Google.

For example, if you are considering starting a business selling logos, you may use the following prompt:

Prompt: "What are [quantity] most popular sub-topics related to [niche business idea]?"

Example: What are 5 most popular sub-topics related to buying logos online?

ChatGPT results (OpenAI, 2023):
As of my knowledge cutoff in September 2021, here are five popular sub-topics related to buying logos online:

1. Logo design marketplaces: Explore the various online platforms that connect businesses with freelance graphic designers or design agencies. These marketplaces offer a wide range of logo design options, allowing you to browse portfolios, compare prices, and hire a designer that suits your needs.
2. Custom logo design: Learn about the process of getting a custom logo designed specifically for your business. This sub-topic covers aspects such as understanding your brand identity, communicating your requirements to the designer, and reviewing design concepts and revisions.
3. Premade logo templates: Discover the concept of premade logo templates, which are pre-designed logos that can be customized with your business name and colors. Explore websites or marketplaces that offer a wide selection of premade logo templates, enabling you to find a design that aligns with your brand quickly.
4. Logo design contests: Explore the idea of hosting a logo design contest where multiple designers compete to create a logo for your business. This subtopic covers platforms that facilitate logo design contests, the process of selecting a winner, and providing feedback to designers during the contest.
5. DIY logo design tools: Learn about online tools and software that allow you to create your own logo without hiring a professional designer. This subtopic covers popular logo design software, their features, and limitations, as well as tips for creating an effective logo using these tools.

Please note that the popularity of sub-topics may change over time, so it's always a good idea to research current trends and platforms in the field of logo design.

Now, you can go a step further and take one of the five subtopics ChatGPT has provided, and create a follow-up prompt. The prompt could be:

Prompt: "What are [quantity] most popular sub-topics, without description, related to [sub-topic]?"

Example: What are 5 most popular sub-topics, without description, related to logo design services?

ChatGPT results (OpenAI, 2023):
Here are five popular sub-topics related to logo design services:

1. Logo design process
2. Logo design pricing
3. Logo design portfolio
4. Logo design trends
5. Logo design tips

You can also create a prompt to gather keywords related to a specific topic. For example, you may be interested to find out what consumers type into Google when looking for logo trends. You would use the following prompt:

Prompt: "List without providing a description, the top [quantity] most popular keywords for [write down specific topic]."

Example: List without providing a description, the top 5 most popular keywords for logo design trends.

ChatGPT results (OpenAI, 2023):

Here are the top 5 most popular keywords for logo design trends:

1. Minimalist logos
2. Flat design logos
3. Vintage logos
4. Geometric logos
5. Hand-drawn logos

If you want longer and more specific keyword phrases, you can use the following prompt:

Prompt: "List without providing a description, the top [quantity] most popular long-tail keywords for [write down specific topic]."

Example: List without providing a description, the top 5 most popular long-tail keywords for logo design trends.

ChatGPT results (OpenAI, 2023):
Here are the top 5 most popular long-tail keywords for logo design trends:

1. Logo design trends for startups
2. Retro logo design trends
3. Modern logo design trends
4. Logo design trends for 2021
5. Logo design trends for small businesses

Another way to use keyword search on ChatGPT is to find out which keywords specific types of customers are searching for. This information can help you identify specific needs of your target audience. Here is an example of a prompt you can use:

Prompt: "List [quantity] long-tail keywords, for the topic of [briefly summarize topic], most commonly searched by [Give a specific target audience]."

Example: List 10 long-tail keywords, for the topic of logo designs, most commonly searched by college students.

ChatGPT results (OpenAI, 2023):
Here are 10 long-tail keywords related to logo designs that are commonly searched by college students:

1. Affordable logo design services for college students
2. Logo design ideas for college projects
3. Creative logo designs for college clubs and organizations
4. Logo design trends for college startups
5. Logo design tips for college students
6. Logo design inspiration for college events
7. Custom logo designs for college merchandise
8. Logo design services for college publications
9. Logo design contests for college students
10. Professional logo design services for college graduates

You can go one step further and ask the chatbot to provide frequently asked questions your target audience may have about the specific topic. You can use the following prompt:

Prompt: "Based on the topic of [topic], list the [quantity] most frequently asked questions by [target audience]."

Example: Based on the topic of purchasing logo designs online, list the 10 most frequently asked questions by college students.

ChatGPT results (OpenAI, 2023):
Here are 10 frequently asked questions by college students regarding purchasing logo designs online:

1. How much does it cost to buy a logo design online?

2. Are there any discounts or special pricing options for college students?

3. Can I get a custom logo design that reflects my college or university's brand?

4. What file formats will I receive when I purchase a logo design online?

5. Can I request revisions or modifications to the logo design if needed?

6. How long does it typically take to receive the final logo design after placing an order?

7. Are there any copyright or ownership issues when buying a logo design online?

8. Can I use the purchased logo design for both personal and commercial purposes?

9. What should I look for in a logo design service or platform to ensure quality and reliability?

10. Are there any specific logo design services or platforms that cater to college students' needs or budgets?

It's important to note that these questions may vary depending on the individual needs and concerns of college students.

You can use the comprehensive information you have gathered from your keyword search to come up with a unique angle for your niche business!

IN SUMMARY

- A niche market refers to unique products and services catering to the needs and interests of a smaller audience. Niche businesses within these markets tend to focus on a single product or service instead of a full range or catalog.

- The benefit of having a niche business is that you can save time and money on production costs, allowing you to reinvest resources in specific areas like sales and marketing.
- ChatGPT can help you identify a niche business idea through skillful keyword searching. Similar to any other SEO tool, the chatbot can collect data on common keywords, phrases, and questions searched by your target audience.

Now that you understand how to find your niche business, let's cross over to the next chapter and look at ways to structure your business model.

CHAPTER 10
CHOOSING YOUR BUSINESS MODEL

Your job as an entrepreneur or executive or project creator is to set things in motion, not do it all yourself!

RICHIE NORTON

WHY ARE ONLINE BUSINESS MODELS POPULAR?

Stop reading for a moment and reflect on how many transactions you complete using your cell phone or laptop.

If you could give an estimate, what percentage of your personal and professional tasks do you complete over the internet or on an app? Think about everyday tasks like buying groceries, transferring money, paying for subscriptions, researching local businesses, booking appointments, getting quotes, and so on.

It has become more common for consumers to make transactions online. Statistics show that 81% of shoppers conduct a background search on a business through the internet before deciding to buy goods from them, and 29.7% of all business in the US is conducted online (compared to 9% back in 2002) (Flynn, 2023).

The reason you may prefer to transact on your mobile device is because it is simple and convenient. You don't need to put gas in your car, drive miles out of your neighborhood, and wait in long lines, only to be told that what you are looking for is out of stock or unavailable. You also don't need to trust a business's word when they claim to be reliable; it is much easier to read online reviews and feedback from their customers.

Since you understand the benefit of online businesses for consumers, you can see why many entrepreneurs are opting for this particular business model. If your number one goal is to make life better for your customers, then why wouldn't you establish an online business? Or at least incorporate technology into your structure?

Of course, success isn't guaranteed regardless of which model you choose. However, some models give you a competitive advantage—and for a startup business, you need as much advantage as you can get! Below are a few benefits of choosing an online business model:

1. Low startup costs

It takes several months to a year for a startup to generate profits. Until then, you will need to inject cash to keep your business running. Having low startup costs means that your business won't require a lot of money to operate each month. For instance, with most online businesses, the biggest costs are building the website or purchasing merchandise. Everything else can be done with free or affordable software.

Some online retail businesses save costs by implementing a dropshipping model. With this model, the entrepreneur acts as a middleman between the shopper and the manufacturing company. When the shipper places an order, the manufacturer is notified and ships the items directly to them. The entrepreneur saves money by not purchasing and keeping stock on hand.

2. Easy to scale

Whenever a physical business grows, they need to move to a bigger office or building, hire more employees, and invest in more sophisticated systems. The difference with online businesses is that they can expand without investing more money. For instance, you don't need to build a new website or hire more employees. You can simply optimize the assets you have and take advantage of technology tools like ChatGPT.

3. Reach more customers

Another benefit of online businesses is the access they have to larger customer bases. There are billions of internet users who browse social media and search engines on a daily basis, and even if your business was able to reach 0.001% of your target audience, that would be 10,000 people. For a startup, having access to 10,000 potential customers is impressive!

Online businesses are not restricted to a physical location, so you are able to do business with customers from across the world. This is more convenient when you are selling digital products that customers can easily download from their web page, instead of dealing with the logistics of shipping.

Maintaining a community is also less strenuous when relationships with customers are built and maintained through digital platforms. All of the admin that comes with customer relationship management, such as sending emails and surveys, responding to queries, scheduling events, or engaging in real-time, can be done with the assistance of AI chatbots.

COMMON TYPES OF ONLINE BUSINESS MODELS

If you are set on starting an online business, your next dilemma could be deciding on which type of online business model to adopt. Bear in mind, this decision won't be simple due to the amount of options you have. As mentioned earlier, your unique value proposition is the anchor to your model, thus always consider it when you are making choices about your business structure.

Below is a list of profitable online business models that can work for your specific business needs. Note that even though these are profitable models, success is not guaranteed. To reduce risk and better your chances of success, consider a business model that best executes your niche business idea, but also fits within your budget and personal lifestyle.

1. Content-based website

A content-based website is a hub for information that may be useful to visitors. The information may be written or shared through audio or video. There are no restrictions to the topics you can explore on your site. However, if you are building a niche business, you may want to focus on specific types of content.

For example, if you are targeting people who are in the process or curious about renovating their homes, your content would be based on information that may be useful on their home improvement journey. The goal is to produce content that solves their problems and makes the process manageable.

There are various ways of generating revenue with content-based websites, such as displaying Google Ads, affiliate marketing, selling add-ons like merchandise or digital products, and promoting sponsored content. Some of the ways to get the word out about your website include sharing content links on social media, optimizing your website content so you are discoverable on search pages, and even running email newsletters and marketing campaigns.

The disadvantage of this model is the amount of time required to produce shareable and optimized content on an ongoing basis. In most cases, your information needs to be well-researched, up-to-date, and even capable of predicting future trends. Not only do you need to create a lot of content, it must be good quality to ensure that people continue to visit your site.

2. E-commerce website

An e-commerce business is the online equivalent of a brick-and-mortar retail store or market. The website will vary in size and service offerings, depending on what is being sold. For example, you could have an e-commerce website that offers different categories of products, or one that sells one category of products. Services can also be sold and either facilitated online or offline.

In terms of time and money, e-commerce websites require more investment than content-based websites. But how much you spend will be determined by the complexity of your structure.

For example, building an online marketplace with various sellers paying commission to list their products or services on your website is niche, but requires a more sophisticated system. You may have to hire a developer to assist you with the setup and functionality of your site, as well as hire staff to help you manage sellers and buyers.

In contrast, an e-commerce website based on a dropshipping model generally requires less investment. You are the only "seller" who interacts with customers, plus the packaging, handling, and delivery of the products are managed by a third-party manufacturing company. The advantage is that you don't have to keep stock on hand, which saves a lot of cash. Many e-commerce hosting platforms, like Shopify, help you set up your dropshipping website and connect you with hundreds of dropshipping services!

3. E-learning website

During the COVID-19 pandemic lockdowns, e-learning websites became popular due to professionals seeking to upgrade their skills, students learning from home, and a growing demand for new knowledge that can help us thrive in the future.

An e-learning website is similar to a content-based website, however, it differs in the way information is packaged. Instead of sharing free content related to ideas, tips, or strategies about a specific topic, e-learning websites monetize information by selling courses, training programs, and webinars.

The convenience factor is that learning can take place at the pace of each student, and access to the learning material is available for a lifetime. For example, even if it takes a student a year to complete a course, due to interruptions in between, they will still be able to monitor their progress and access learning materials. Some e-learning websites offer free courses, but these typically don't come with verification, such as a certificate of completion. The learning material provided may also be restricted until the student pays.

One of the most recent and growing trends in e-learning is the use of AI tools for assisted learning. For example, instead of having a language instructor when you are teaching a language, you can incorporate an interactive chatbot that helps language students with questions, quizzes, and practical assessments. AI can also provide students with real-time tracking of their progress and identify areas where they can improve.

Similar to content-based websites, you will need to invest a lot of resources into producing high-quality courses and other digital learning products. Moreover, visitors may want to see proof that your learning material is credible and verifiable.

For example, publishing a course created by a chatbot will not fare well with students. They expect to learn from industry experts, entrepreneurs with a proven track record, or reputable educational institutions.

Other technical aspects of producing digital products, such as content creation and editing, may require a lot of money to achieve a quality product. Nevertheless, the benefit of digital products is that you make a once-off investment and can sell it hundreds of times. Thus, after some time, you will make the money back.

Out of these three models, it is difficult to say which is the best because it depends on your niche and specific needs. Any of these models can work for you, provided you have a compelling and unique value proposition.

If you are planning on doing freelance work, a simple website, such as a personal blog, introducing who you are and showcasing your skills can work! Your website doesn't need to be too sophisticated since your tasks will be completed using third-party sites and apps. Another great option is to register a freelancer account on bidding sites like Fiverr and Upwork. Both of these platforms allow you to build a comprehensive profile, upload a portfolio of work, set your price per hour, and connect with clients looking for freelancers.

HOW TO FIND THE RIGHT BUSINESS MODEL USING CHATGPT

If you are unsure about which online business model is right for you, it may be useful to consult with ChatGPT. As mentioned previously, the quality of your prompts will determine the quality of your search results. Thus, instead of typing "List the best online business model" you can generate more specific prompts that are related to your business idea or needs.

Here are a few prompt suggestions you can try:

Prompt: Identify [quantity] of the best online business models for [type of product or service you will be offering].

Example: Identify two of the best online business models for writing services.

ChatGPT results (OpenAI, 2023):
Two of the best online business models for writing services are:

1. Freelance Writing Platforms: Freelance writing platforms provide a marketplace where writers can offer their services and clients can hire them for various writing projects. These platforms act as intermediaries, connecting clients with writers and handling the payment and administrative processes. Popular freelance writing platforms include Upwork, Freelancer, and Fiverr. As a writer, you can create a profile, showcase your skills and expertise, bid on projects, and build a client base. This model offers flexibility, as you can choose the projects you want to work on, set your own rates, and work remotely.

2. Content Creation Agencies: Content creation agencies operate as professional writing services that offer a wide range of writing solutions to businesses and individuals. They typically have a team of writers with diverse expertise and can handle projects of varying sizes and complexity. Content creation agencies often provide services such as blog writing, website content development, copywriting, editing, and proofreading. As an agency, you can build long-term relationships with clients, provide consistent quality, and scale your operations. Marketing and networking play a crucial role in acquiring clients and establishing your agency's reputation.

Both of these models have their advantages and can be successful depending on your preferences and business goals. It's essential to consider factors such as your writing skills, marketing abilities, available resources, and target audience when choosing the most suitable model for your writing services.

You can also ask ChatGPT to suggest the best business model that would fit your startup budget. Consider the example below:

Prompt: I have [startup budget]. What is the best business model for me?

Example: I have $500. What is the best business model for me?

ChatGPT results (OpenAI, 2023):

Determining the best business model for you requires careful consideration of your skills, interests, market trends, and personal goals. While I can't make an exact recommendation without knowing more about you, I can provide you with some popular business models that you could explore. Here are a few options to consider:

1. E-commerce Store: Use your $500 to set up an online store and sell products or services. You can leverage platforms like Shopify or Etsy to start your business. Research market trends and identify a niche or product that has demand.
2. Freelancing: If you have a specific skill set, such as graphic design, writing, programming, or social media management, you can offer your services as a freelancer. Create a professional portfolio, join freelancing platforms like Upwork or Fiverr, and start marketing your skills.
3. Dropshipping: With dropshipping, you can set up an online store without managing inventory. You market and sell products, but the supplier handles the storage and shipping. Research profitable products and work with reliable suppliers to ensure smooth operations.
4. Content Creation: If you enjoy creating content, you can start a blog, YouTube channel, or podcast. Monetize your content through advertising, sponsorships, or affiliate marketing. Consistency and quality are crucial for building an audience.
5. Consulting: If you have expertise in a particular field, consider offering consulting services. Identify a target market that needs your knowledge and skills, and offer your expertise through one-on-one sessions, workshops, or online courses.

Remember, starting a business involves more than just choosing a business model. Conduct thorough market research, develop a business plan, and assess your competition before investing your money. It's also crucial to adapt and refine your business as you gain experience and feedback from customers.

Remember that these are suggestions based on the chatbot's pretrained data, which cuts off in 2021. This means that what was a good business model back then may not be as popular today. The results generated by ChatGPT should therefore serve as a guideline, rather than the final decision. Take the information you are given and verify it with current market trends and research.

IN SUMMARY

- A business model is the structure of your business that enables you to generate revenue. There isn't a fixed rule on which model to choose; the decision rests on your niche business idea, unique value proposition, and startup budget.
- Online business models are fast becoming a popular choice for entrepreneurs and freelancers because of how affordable, flexible, and scalable they are. Three main types of online business models out there are content-based websites, e-commerce websites, and e-learning websites.
- If you are struggling to choose the right business model for you, consult ChatGPT. Generate prompts specific to your business needs and see what comes up. Since the chatbot's database cuts off in 2021, be sure to compare your results with current market trends and research.

Now that you understand how to choose an online business model, we'll soon look at ways to conduct market research with the assistance of ChatGPT.

INSPIRE OTHERS TO DOUBLE THEIR INCOME WITH THE INSIGHT OF CHATGPT!

"The measure of intelligence is the ability to change"

ALBERT EINSTEIN

Job unhappiness is at a staggering all-time high, according to a recent Gallup poll, and millions of workers are leaving their job every month—despite fears of a slowing economy and recession!

There is no doubt that 2020 completely changed the zeitgeist—and the way we view work and quality of life. It was as though the trauma of that year sparked a mind shift that resulted in many refusing to be a slave to the 9 to 5 machine. Thanks to ubiquitous connectivity and powerful AI tools, you can literally work from anywhere in the world—and you don't need to wait to do so, or invest thousands of dollars in a fancy new post-grad degree.

Within this vastly changing panorama, one tool that has revolutionized the world of freelance work and entrepreneurship is ChatGPT. By this stage of your reading, you know that the number of applications this tool has is mind-blowing. From content creation to investment, starting a business to generating code or financial solutions, ChatGPT is changing how we work and knocking down an immeasurable number of obstacles.

You have seen how ChatGPT can help you start a small business with as little as $100. You have additionally discovered a host of useful prompts you can use to receive a myriad of ideas for everything from your website content to how to find the right niche and set up an online business. You realize that ChatGPT could be the way out of the daily grind and the way into more lucrative, less time-consuming work.

If this book inspires you to embark on your own journey as a freelance worker, content creator, or entrepreneur, I would love it if you reviewed it on Amazon. Feel free to share a couple of quick insights on what you found most useful.

By leaving a review of this book on Amazon, you'll show other readers that they don't have to give into the fear of financial instability and job loss—they can become their own boss as of right now.

Encourage others to move beyond passive acceptance of a life they aren't content with, to one that aligns more closely with their values.

Your words will help them discover that with ChatGPT on their side, they can supplement their income through freelance work or make their first forays into entrepreneurship.

Scan the QR-code below to go directly to the review page.

CHAPTER 11
CONDUCTING MARKET RESEARCH ONLINE

Without data, you're just another person with an opinion.

EDWARD DEMING

WHAT IS MARKET RESEARCH?

Market research is the process of collecting data to assess the success of a potential business idea. This process is typically undertaken during the early stages of forming a company, around the same time you put together a business plan. You don't need to be an expert data scientist to perform market research. For the most part, everything you are looking for is already accessible online. The information you gather can be used to help you make certain business decisions, such as

- identifying and analyzing a specific target audience.
- researching product or service offerings.
- formulating a marketing and sales strategy.
- formulating a pricing strategy.
- finding the most suitable social media platforms.

- completing a competitor analysis.
- discovering untapped business opportunities.

A survey compiled by a marketing firm called Attest showed that over a quarter (26%) of entrepreneurs do not perform market research before launching their businesses. Of those who didn't perform market research, some of their reasons included not being able to afford it (21%) and believing that it is a waste of time (35%). What was surprising, however, is that 75% of respondents admitted that they don't fully understand their target audience (Fresh Business Thinking, 2016).

Could it be that the reason why some entrepreneurs fail to engage their target audiences is due to not investing enough time in market research? It is very risky to assume that you understand the needs of customers without going through the process of gaining insights. The risk is even greater when you are catering to customers with different life paths. For example, Gen Zers may expect something more unique from businesses compared to millennials or Gen Xers.

Market research is a crucial step in the formation of your business. After going through the steps and gathering relevant information, you will be able to answer critical questions about who you are as a business, what you offer, how you serve customers, what makes you stand out, and why your products or services matter. It also gives you an opportunity to get to know the people you intend on converting to customers and the kinds of needs or problems they might have. Once you understand their problems, you can come up with a desired solution that makes life easier for them and complements their lifestyle.

To give you an idea of the questions answered through market research, here are a few examples:

- Who is your target audience? Where are they? What do they need most?

- Which competitors are currently serving your target audience? What are their strengths and weaknesses?
- What are the latest trends in your industry? How have consumer purchasing behaviors evolved?
- Is there a demand for the products or services you will be offering? If so, how big is the demand?
- How much are customers willing to pay for products or services similar to yours?

It is common for entrepreneurs to start businesses wearing rose-colored glasses, especially when they are passionate about the idea. As a result, they are unable to scrutinize their business models and look out for blind spots. Market research reduces the risk of biases or making unfounded assumptions, so you can see the business for what it is, instead of what you imagine it could be.

MARKET RESEARCH METHODS

There are two main methods to conduct market research: primary and secondary research. Think of these methods as two branches that grow from the same tree. Both methods are useful depending on what type of information you are looking for.

Primary research is information that comes directly from the source, which could be an individual or company representative. In some cases, you will need to pay money to access this kind of information, since the individual or institution owns full rights to their data.

The process of compiling primary research can also require time and money. For example, you may need to send out a proposal and set of questions to request an interview, compensate the interviewee for their time and data, transcribe the interview, then extract insights. Or maybe you would like to host an online focus group with members of your target audience. Each participant would need to sign a consent form, agree to meet online at a specific date and time, and they would need to be compensated in some way too.

On the other hand, secondary research is information found online through blogs, social media, journals, and industry websites. It may or may not be credible depending on the source. For example, an article published on a website like Harvard Business Review may be more factually correct than an article published on a gossip site. It is also advised to fact-check the information you collect online to ensure that you are citing accurate figures and statistics.

Compared with primary research, secondary research is more affordable and accessible. You may not also need to get consent from individuals or institutions before using the information unless, of course, they require that you do. Furthermore, while most research is free, there are some educational platforms that require you to pay a subscription for access to their database of articles, books, and research papers.

Below are examples of sites you can visit to access secondary research:

- trade and industry associations
- company websites
- social media platforms
- blogs and media outlets
- online libraries
- competitor websites
- government agencies

From the two research methods, there are tools that you can use to collect information. These are known as qualitative and quantitative research tools. Once again, the tool you end up choosing will depend on the kind of information you need. For example, qualitative research tools collect information about customer sentiments, attitudes, and behavior. They seek to understand how certain business processes or products affect customers.

Examples of qualitative research tools are

- interviews
- focus groups
- qualitative surveys
- observational tools
- product/service trials
- hypothesis testing
- ethnographic tools

Quantitative research tools focus on facts and figures. The goal of collecting information is to analyze data and identify patterns. Instead of ending up with insights after the research process, your results will come in numerical format, such as a percentage or average. Other uses for quantitative research tools are to spot trends, make predictions about the future, or analyze the performance of your business compared to competitors.

Examples of quantitative research tools are

- quantitative surveys
- questionnaires
- probability samplings
- online polls
- biometrics

FIVE STEPS TO COMPLETE MARKET RESEARCH

If you have completed any form of research in the past, you will know that it can be a strenuous process. To make your market research move swiftly, look at it as a project with several steps. Don't attempt to undertake multiple tasks at once; this will only tire you out early and lower your motivation to continue. Instead, focus on one step at a time, and each small research task within the step. It is also good to give yourself enough time to complete the steps, taking into consideration your busy schedule.

When you are ready to start with your market research, here are the steps to follow:

1. Create clear objectives

Before you start surfing the internet, have a goal in mind about what you would like to achieve. It is not possible to research everything about your chosen market, industry, or customers in one go, hence the need for clear objectives. For each session, plan out the following:

- what type of information you are looking for
- how much time you need to set aside to look for the information
- the most appropriate research method and tools
- various sites and sources that might have the information you need
- key metrics that will confirm you have found the right information

If possible, write down your objectives as SMART statements, ensuring that they are specific, measurable, achievable, relevant, and time-bound. Writing out your objectives allows you to clarify your goal and have something to constantly refer to.

2. Choose the most appropriate research method

Another reason why you should write your objectives down is so you are able to determine what research method is appropriate. Remember, the research method you choose will be determined by the type of information you are looking for.

For example, primary research would be appropriate if you wanted feedback from potential customers, whereas secondary research would be appropriate if you wanted to analyze consumer trends and behaviors. After you have chosen the best research method, it will be easier to identify suitable research tools (i.e. whether to draw up a qualitative survey or read the latest market trends report online).

3. Prepare the necessary research tools

Before you can perform research, you will need to prepare your research tools. This means creating a simple brief that explains your objective for using the tool, the sample size (if you are going to include research participants), the plan for finding the participants, the process you will take them through, and the resources you will need to successfully complete the project. At minimum, you will need to have a research objective and a framework of how you are going to use the tool.

4. Carry out your research

The fourth step will be straightforward, as long as you have done the necessary preparations. Essentially, all you have to do is start! Your research plan will tell you where to look for information, what to look for, who to consult for help, and so on. The only task is to stick as close as possible to your research plan and follow the guidelines. For example, if you had decided on conducting interviews with 10 people, follow through by contacting the relevant people and requesting an interview. Have your email scripts ready so that you don't have to think about what you are going to say.

Time management is also crucial when conducting research. Note that spending more time on the internet won't necessarily ensure better results. The aim is to use your time efficiently and collect the data you need, without getting distracted. To keep yourself accountable to the set time frame, you can set up weekly check-ins to review the information you have found and set targets for the following week.

5. Analyze the data

Many people assume that they are finished after collecting information, however, there is still a final step to perform—analyzing the data. This step is important to ensure you extract key points or insights from the data. What makes it tedious is the fact that each research tool will have its own framework for summarizing data and extracting key points or insights. For example, how you analyze interviews won't be the same as how you analyze questionnaires.

During your preparation of research tools, write down an outline of how you are going to analyze the data collected. For example, are you going to identify and categorize themes that are uncovered from an interview, or will you draw up pie charts to summarize survey data? Research a few ways to analyze your data and choose the option that brings the most value to your market research.

HOW TO USE CHATGPT FOR MARKET RESEARCH

At this point, you have all of the information required to get started with your market research. But how can we end the chapter without showing you how to use ChatGPT to conduct market research? After all, this book is all about leveraging AI support in starting and maintaining profitable businesses!

So far, you have seen evidence of ChatGPT assisting with many personal and professional tasks, and market research is no exception. Some of the impressive tasks the chatbot can perform include setting research goals, creating a comprehensive research plan, and collecting and analyzing data. It can even perform more advanced tasks, such as conducting a competitor analysis and building customer personas.

Below are some market research prompts that you can use for your upcoming business project:

Prompt: I want to start a business [explain business concept briefly]. Please provide me with the core data on the industry, in less than 200 words.

Example: I want to start a business selling print-on-demand t-shirts online. Please provide me with the core data on the industry, keep it very short.

ChatGPT results (OpenAI, 2023):
The print-on-demand t-shirt industry is a segment of the e-commerce market that allows businesses to create custom-designed t-shirts on-demand. It involves printing designs on blank t-shirts only after an order is received, eliminating the need for inventory. The industry has experienced significant growth due to its low startup costs, flexibility in design options, and ease of entry into the market. Major players in the industry include platforms like Printful, Printify, and CustomInk. Successful businesses in this industry focus on unique designs, effective marketing strategies, and maintaining quality production and customer service.

You can also ask the chatbot to complete a competitor analysis for you, using the prompt below:

Prompt: As a startup [write down the niche you are in] business, who would be my two biggest competitors? Identify the strengths and weaknesses of each competitor. Your response should be less than 200 words.

Example: As a startup print-on-demand business, who would be my two biggest competitors? Identify the strengths and weaknesses of each competitor. Your response should be less than 200 words.

ChatGPT results (OpenAI, 2023):
As a startup print-on-demand business, two major competitors in

the industry are Printful and Printify. Here are their strengths and weaknesses:

1. Printful:

- Strengths: Printful is a popular and well-established platform with a wide range of product offerings beyond t-shirts. They have a user-friendly interface and seamless integration with major e-commerce platforms. Printful offers high-quality printing, reliable fulfillment, and excellent customer support. They also have an extensive network of printing facilities worldwide, allowing for efficient shipping.
- Weaknesses: Printful's pricing structure can be relatively higher compared to other competitors, which can impact profit margins. They also have limited customization options for some products, leading to less design flexibility. Additionally, since Printful is widely used, it can be challenging to differentiate your brand and stand out from competitors who use the same platform.

2. Printify:

- Strengths: Printify offers a large selection of print providers, allowing businesses to choose the best fit for their needs. They have competitive pricing options, offering potential cost savings for startups. Printify provides a user-friendly interface and easy integration with various e-commerce platforms. They also offer a wide range of customizable products, providing more design flexibility.
- Weaknesses: Compared to Printful, Printify's customer support may be less responsive and sometimes slower in addressing inquiries. Although they offer numerous print providers, the quality of printing and fulfillment can vary depending on the chosen provider. This inconsistency in quality can pose a challenge when ensuring a consistent customer experience.

To succeed as a startup, it's crucial to differentiate your brand by focusing on unique designs, excellent marketing strategies, and delivering exceptional customer service. Additionally, consider exploring other niche or specialized print-on-demand providers to further distinguish your business from these major competitors.

If you have not identified a target audience yet, ChatGPT can help you create one! Here is an example of a prompt that can pull relevant information on potential customers:

Prompt: I am starting a [write down the niche you are in] business. Please help me identify a target audience. For example, identify the demographics of people who would be interested in my business. Give an explanation why they are the right audience.

> Example: I am starting a print-on-demand business. Please help me identify a target audience. For example, identify the demographics of people who would be interested in my business. Give an explanation why they are the right audience.

> ChatGPT results (OpenAI, 2023):
> Based on the nature of your print-on-demand business, the target audience can vary depending on your chosen niche and design focus. However, a general target audience that could be interested in your business includes:

> 1. Creative Professionals and Artists:

> - Demographics: This audience may consist of graphic designers, illustrators, photographers, and artists of various mediums.
> - Explanation: Creative professionals and artists often appreciate unique and customizable products that allow them to express their creativity and showcase their work. They may be interested in your business for custom-designed t-shirts featuring their own

artwork or designs. By catering to this audience, you can tap into a niche market and build a loyal customer base. Consider offering design collaboration options or artist partnerships to further attract and engage this audience.

2. Small Business Owners and Entrepreneurs:

- Demographics: Small business owners and entrepreneurs across different industries, such as startups, online businesses, and local brands.
- Explanation: Small business owners and entrepreneurs are often looking for cost-effective ways to promote their brand and create merchandise without investing in large-scale production or inventory. Your print-on-demand service provides them with the flexibility to create custom t-shirts featuring their logos, slogans, or unique designs in small quantities or on-demand. Emphasize the convenience, affordability, and scalability of your services to appeal to this audience.

3. Social Causes and Nonprofit Organizations:

- Demographics: Individuals involved in social causes, activists, nonprofit organizations, and community groups.
- Explanation: Social causes and nonprofit organizations often rely on merchandise sales to raise awareness, funds, and support for their causes. Your print-on-demand business can provide them with a hassle-free solution for creating custom t-shirts that feature their mission, slogans, or artwork. By aligning your business with social causes, you can attract a passionate and dedicated audience that values the impact of their purchases and seeks to support meaningful initiatives.

Remember, it's essential to conduct thorough market research and validate your target audience through surveys, competitor analysis, and customer feedback. This will help you refine your target audience based on their preferences, purchasing behavior, and needs specific to your print-on-demand business.

You can go a step further and ask ChatGPT to create a detailed audience persona for the target audience you have identified. Consider this follow-up prompt and its results:

Prompt: Create a detailed audience persona for the target audience mentioned above. Include key information, such as audience likes and dislikes, and common challenges faced related to print-on-demand businesses.

ChatGPT results (OpenAI, 2023):
Audience Persona: Creative Claire

Background:
Claire is a 28-year-old graphic designer and freelance illustrator. She has a bachelor's degree in graphic design and has been working in the creative industry for five years. Claire is passionate about art and enjoys expressing her creativity through various mediums. She is always looking for opportunities to showcase her artwork and designs to a broader audience.

Likes:

1. Customization: Claire loves products that can be personalized and customized, allowing her to add her artistic touch to them.
2. Quality Printing: She values high-quality printing that accurately represents the colors and details of her artwork.
3. Collaboration: Claire enjoys collaborating with other artists and creative individuals to explore new design ideas and styles.

4. Convenience: She appreciates services that are easy to use and integrate seamlessly with her online portfolio and e-commerce platforms.
5. Social Impact: Claire is drawn to brands that support social causes and contribute positively to the community.

Dislikes:

1. Limited Design Options: Claire dislikes platforms with limited design tools or constraints that hinder her creative expression.
2. Poor Customer Support: She gets frustrated with slow or unresponsive customer support when facing technical or printing issues.
3. Inconsistent Printing Quality: Claire is disappointed when her artwork doesn't come out as expected due to printing inconsistencies.
4. Complicated Order Process: She finds it bothersome to navigate complex and time-consuming order processes.

Challenges related to print-on-demand businesses:

1. Design Compatibility: Claire faces challenges in ensuring her artwork meets the required design specifications for printing on different apparel types and sizes.
2. Pricing and Profit Margins: As an independent artist, Claire needs to balance competitive pricing for her custom t-shirts while maintaining reasonable profit margins.
3. Branding and Differentiation: She struggles to stand out in a crowded market and effectively brand her print-on-demand products to attract a loyal customer base.
4. Inventory Management: Claire wants to avoid the burden of managing inventory, making print-on-demand an attractive solution.

5. Sustainable Practices: As an environmentally conscious individual, Claire seeks print-on-demand providers that prioritize eco-friendly printing options.

As a print-on-demand business owner, you can tailor your services to cater to Creative Claire's needs by providing:

1. Robust Design Tools: Offer an intuitive and feature-rich design tool that allows Claire to create and customize her t-shirts with ease.
2. Responsive Customer Support: Ensure a responsive and helpful customer support team that assists her promptly in case of any issues.
3. High-Quality Printing: Partner with reliable printing facilities to deliver consistent, high-quality prints that accurately portray her artwork.
4. User-Friendly Platform Integration: Integrate your services seamlessly with popular e-commerce platforms and website builders, simplifying her order process.
5. Eco-Friendly Printing Options: Offer eco-conscious printing choices and highlight your commitment to sustainability, appealing to Claire's values.

By understanding and addressing the needs of Creative Claire, you can effectively target and attract creative professionals like her to become loyal customers for your print-on-demand business.

The possibilities for the type of market research data you can generate from ChatGPT are endless. The main difference between using the AI chatbot and sourcing information from a range of sites on the internet is that you don't need to manually summarize and analyze the information. ChatGPT can do that for you! Plus, since the chatbot is going through thousands of data entries to find the information you need, you might get better quality results using it.

IN SUMMARY

- Market research is the process of verifying the profitability of your business by seeing whether there is a market for it. It can also be used to identify the ideal target audience, industry competitors, and the latest consumer trends and analytics.
- There are five steps to undertake when performing market research. These steps include creating clear objectives, choosing the most appropriate research method, creating a plan for your research tools, conducting the research, and analyzing the data.
- If you are looking to save time and potentially collect more relevant and quality information, you can turn to ChatGPT. The chatbot can assist you with various market research needs, such as summarizing industry trends, identifying competitors, and creating a target audience persona.

Now that you understand how to conduct market research, let's cross over to the next chapter and look at how you can use ChatGPT to compile a business plan.

CHAPTER 12
CREATING A BUSINESS PLAN FOR YOUR ONLINE BUSINESS

Without a plan, even the most brilliant business can get lost. You need to have goals, create milestones and have a strategy in place to set yourself up for success.

YOGI BERRA

WHAT IS A BUSINESS PLAN?

The software company, Palo Alto Software, invited over 3,000 business owners to complete a survey. The survey asked a range of questions related to their business models, goals, and planning. The results from the survey showed that business owners who took the time to draft and complete their business plans were twice as likely to grow their businesses and secure loans and investments than business owners who didn't (Berry, 2010).

There is no doubt that you need a business plan to establish a solid business, however, you may not see the point in creating one. Business plans have been historically seen as company documents that you complete once and shove into a filing cabinet, never to access again. Entrepreneurs created them just to tick a box, instead of using them as a guideline for starting and growing their businesses. Some may have even added generic information to rush the process and submit to a financial institution for funding, only to realize later on that the joke was on them!

Yes, it is true that business plans are company documents. However, they are supposed to be referred to and updated as you overcome challenges or identify new opportunities. Even though they don't guarantee the success of your business, they can keep you focused on specific tasks and processes that help your business grow.

Business plans specifically designed for online businesses will include the following information:

- **Digital location instead of a physical building address.** Since your business is hosted on a website, it will have a URL or website address. When referring to the "location" of your business, you will mention this information, as well as other locations your brand can be found online, such as social media accounts.
- **Global competitor analysis instead of local competitor analysis.** With your business based online, the competition gets a lot steeper. Not only do you need to consider the local brick-and-mortar store selling similar products, but you must also think about companies overseas that could be your direct competitors.
- **Digital-related product and service strengths and weaknesses.** If you are looking to sell digital products or services through your website or online platforms, you will need to consider the challenges that may come with making transactions with customers, such as encountering a system failure, a security breach, or content that doesn't upload correctly.
- **Mainly digital marketing strategies.** It is quite rare for online businesses to have a presence outside of the internet because most of your advertising and promotions take place online. You will notice that your marketing strategy considers digital

channels, such as email, website, social media, and affiliate websites. The upside to this is that the costs of advertising your business through online channels are more affordable than offline channels like TV and radio.

WHAT TO INCLUDE IN YOUR BUSINESS PLAN

When you are ready to draft your business plan, you will need access to a word processor like Microsoft Word, Google Docs, or Evernote. Since this is a formal company document, how you present the information is more important than the design or style of the document. Including elements like a front page, table of contents, sections and subsections, and bibliography will help you stay organized.

Below are ideas of sections that you can include and expand on in your business plan. Nevertheless, your business model will determine the most important components of your business.

1. Executive summary

The executive summary is a one-page summary of your business plan. Most of the time, it is the first bit of information investors will read. Depending on how compelling it is, they may choose to turn the page and find out more about your business. Since there is a lot riding on the executive summary, it is recommended to draft it last, after you have completed the other sections. Examples of what to include in your summary are a brief business overview, the big idea you would like to present, the need you are addressing, and what gives your business a competitive advantage.

2. Company description

The company description is an overview of your company name, mission, and goals. It is one of the few opportunities you will get to sell your business, without seeming boastful! How you write this section is important because it conveys the personality of your business. As such, pay attention to the language, tone of voice, and style of writing that you use. Every piece of information you include should tell a story about who you are and how you hope to make a positive contribution to the market. Key information to include in this section is the mission statement, goals and objectives, brand elements, and company values.

3. Environmental analysis

The environmental analysis looks at the market you will be operating in, and the various factors impacting your business. There are three broad subsections you can include: competitor analysis, licensing and legislation, and technology. Competitor analysis would analyze your direct and indirect competitors, identifying their strengths and weaknesses. You could also complete a SWOT analysis of your business, in comparison to your competitors.

Depending on the type of business you are operating, you might also need to obtain certain licenses or meet legal requirements. At the minimum, if you plan on selling products or services online, you will need to obtain a tax license. The e-commerce industry in the US is regulated by a few governing bodies, such as the Federal Trade Commission. However, there may also be local laws you need to comply with.

Lastly, technology is a major component of your business since it is based online. It is important to assess what technologies you will be competing with, the type of software being released in the market, and the main tech tools you will need to operate your business on an ongoing basis. Consider how much knowledge you have about the technologies your business will operate on, and whether you may need to upskill yourself (or the team who will be helping you).

4. Products and services

The products and services section looks at what you will be selling and the entire process of production, packaging, and promotion. Something that you will need to clarify in this section is the need or problem that your products or services respond to. The clearer you make this, the easier you will find coming up with a unique value proposition.

Plus, customers will want to know what makes your products or services better than other businesses. Lastly, you can discuss the pricing strategy you will use, and what your profit margins will be. Remember, pricing too low might cause cash flow problems, but pricing too high might scare customers away.

5. Marketing plan

The marketing plan is a strategy that explains how you are going to sell products and services. Your plan should have clear goals and objectives, as well as a number of tactics that you will employ to reach target audiences. For example, in the beginning, your goal may be to raise awareness of your business, and to do that, one of your objectives could be to create social media pages so you can connect with your target audience and guide them to your website.

Note that your marketing plan can be short-term or long-term. It is also flexible enough to allow for experimentation. For example, you may want to test the performance of two different ads to see which one customers respond to. Or you may decide to deactivate a social media account when data reveals that not many target audience members are active on that site. Lastly, mention the different tactics that you will use to achieve marketing objectives, such as email marketing, social media advertising, affiliate marketing, and so on.

6. Operations plan

The operations plan looks at the day-to-day running of your business. In particular, it focuses on the different processes or systems that will be operating to make sure that everything is functioning smoothly. For example, you can consider factors like how many employees you will need to hire, what your work schedule will look like, the step-by-step buying process, the returns management process, managing customer queries, and so on. When outlining your processes, assess whether they are efficient (i.e. can be completed in the shortest amount of time and with the smallest amount of money). Find ways to scale your business by automating repetitive tasks and investing in turnkey software.

7. Financial plan

Apart from the executive summary, investors are interested in your business's numbers. The purpose of the financial plan is to illustrate how your business will make profits and remain sustainable in the long run. The types of financial documents to draw up and include in this section are the profit/loss statement, cash flow statement, and balance sheet statement. Many of the figures you add to these statements will be predictions; however, ensure that they are conservative predictions based on verified secondary research, like recent industry forecasts, the inflation rate, and so on.

8. Funding application

Not every business will need funding, but if yours does, your business plan will end with this section. A funding application consists of a few paragraphs where you state the amount of money you are requesting and how you plan on using the money. The more detailed you are, the less room you leave for follow-up questions. It may also help to paint a picture of the future and show the investor how their money will lead to the positive growth of your business. Furthermore, attach supporting documents, like quotes, letters from potential suppliers, or analytics from your social media, which can make your proposal more credible.

CREATE YOUR BUSINESS PLAN WITH CHATGPT

One of the ways entrepreneurs take the pain out of creating business plans is to ask ChatGPT to do it for them! Of course, the answers generated may need to be refined to match your business needs. But for the most part, the chatbot can create a comprehensive plan that is structured and professional in a fraction of the time!

The first prompt that you will need to use to get the process started is requesting an outline for your business plan. An example would be:

Prompt: I am starting a [write down type of business] business. Please provide an outline, without descriptions, for my business plan.

Example: I am starting a podcasting business. Please provide an outline, without descriptions, for my business plan.

ChatGPT results (OpenAI, 2023):

1. Executive Summary
   a. Overview of the podcasting business
   b. Mission statement
   c. Business goals and objectives
2. Business Description
   a. Introduction to the podcasting industry
   b. Target audience and market analysis
   c. Competitive analysis
   d. Unique selling proposition
3. Products and Services
   a. Description of podcasting services offered
   b. Podcast format and content strategy
   c. Monetization strategies
4. Marketing and Sales
   a. Branding and positioning
   b. Marketing strategies and tactics

      c. Audience growth and engagement plans

      d. Collaboration and partnerships

   5. Operations and Management

      a. Team structure and roles

      b. Equipment and technology requirements

      c. Production and editing processes

      d. Quality control measures

   6. Financial Planning

      a. Startup costs and funding sources

      b. Revenue streams and pricing models

      c. Sales projections and financial forecasts

      d. Budgeting and cost management

   7. Legal Considerations

      a. Business structure and registration

      b. Intellectual property protection

      c. Licensing and copyright issues

   8. Risk Analysis

      a. Identification of potential risks and challenges

      b. Mitigation strategies

      c. Contingency plans

   9. Growth and Expansion

      a. Long-term vision and goals

      b. Scaling strategies

      c. Diversification opportunities

   10. Conclusion

      a. Recap of the business plan

      b. Call to action for implementation

      c. Summary of expected outcomes and impact

After receiving an outline, you can go through each section, asking the chatbot to provide an overview, detailed descriptions, or entire plans. To illustrate how this can be achieved, we can ask ChatGPT to create an executive summary of the podcasting business mentioned above, using only 100 words (note that this would be a follow-up question under the same chat, not an entirely new chat):

> Example: Based on the outline provided, complete a draft of the executive summary, using only 100 words. Mention that the business was started by Katie and her husband Steve in their basement studio.

> ChatGPT results (OpenAI, 2023):

> Executive Summary:
> Katie and Steve, co-founders of the podcasting business, have established a dynamic venture in their basement studio. With a mission to inspire and inform, the business aims to captivate a diverse audience through engaging and thought-provoking podcasts. By offering high-quality content across various genres, the business seeks to position itself as a prominent player in the podcasting industry. Through strategic marketing and partnerships, they will foster audience growth and monetization opportunities. With meticulous planning, efficient operations, and a commitment to excellence, Katie and Steve are poised to achieve their business goals and carve out a successful niche in the ever-expanding podcasting landscape.

You can go through the business plan, asking the chatbot to assist you with drafting certain sections!

IN SUMMARY

- A business plan is a company document that outlines the activities of the business and how it will make revenue. Some entrepreneurs choose to go without a business plan, but research shows that their businesses don't grow as steadily or receive as many loans or investments as those that followed a business plan.

- Business plans specifically designed for online businesses focus on answering questions, such as *how will the business survive and compete in the digital landscape?*
- There are various sections to include in your business plan. With the option of AI assistance, you get to choose how many of these sections you would like to draft alone or with the help of ChatGPT.

Now that you understand how to compile a business plan using Chat-GPT, let's cross over to Part 5 and look at how this amazing chatbot can help you perform everyday business tasks.

PART FIVE
THE ACTUAL BUSINESS

CHAPTER 13
BUILDING YOUR ONLINE PRESENCE

We have technology, finally, that for the first time in human history allows people to really maintain rich connections with much larger numbers of people.

PIERRE OMIDYAR

WHY DOES A STRONG ONLINE PRESENCE MATTER?

For online businesses, having an online presence is essential. And this doesn't mean simply building a website or creating social media accounts. An online presence is the image that customers have about your business based on the content you share online. Therefore, building an online presence is as much about reputation management as it is about taking advantage of as many digital channels as possible.

Apart from being discoverable, having an online presence makes your business appear legitimate. For instance, when customers search your name, they are able to see various indications that your business exists. Many will also expect to see customer reviews about your products or services, and as many as 49% of customers need to see a four-star rating before doing business with you (reviews with one or two-star ratings made 86% of prospective customers turn away) (Campbell, 2023).

It takes a startup business some time to build an online presence. These efforts can be accelerated by creating and sharing SEO-friendly content. As you develop new channels and reach out to your target audience, your brand will become recognizable, at least to those few people who have engaged with your content. Your job is to make sure that the information shared about your business is relevant, meaningful, and leaves a good impression on the minds of prospective customers.

HOW TO INCREASE YOUR ONLINE PRESENCE

Like any other marketing initiative, you will need to draw up a plan to increase your online presence. Your plan should start with a clear goal of what you would like to achieve through your online presence. If possible, stick to one goal per quarter or biannually, so you can produce content with the same objective in mind, and measure the growth of your business in a specific area.

Here are examples of goals to set for building an online presence:

- to increase awareness of the business in the minds of the target audience
- to educate the target audience on business offerings, or how to make a purchase
- to add more social proof to the business so prospective customers feel comfortable transacting with us
- to expand reach and connect with more prospective customers

Keep your goals at the back of your mind when you are implementing different tactics to build your online presence. You are welcome to test a wide range of tactics before settling on those that are most effective in achieving your goal.

Here is a list of the type of tactics you can include in your strategy:

1. Build a professional website

Even if most of your interactions with customers occur on social media, it is still important to have a "home" for your business on the internet. Your website serves as a hub that stores every piece of information about your business. Links that you post on different social media sites or websites direct internet users to your website, where they can learn more about what you do. To make your website discoverable on Google, make sure it is optimized, user-friendly, integrates a chatbot, and has clear contact information.

2. Create a business blog

Some businesses incorporate a blog as an extension of their website, while others choose to have a dedicated website to post shareable content. It is up to you to decide whether you need both websites or only one. For instance, freelancers may benefit from having a blogging site rather than a professional website to showcase their content and services. If you are going to create a blog, ensure that every content piece is optimized and includes highly-searched keywords.

3. Regularly ask for reviews and testimonials

Social proofing is a psychological concept that suggests that people are encouraged to take action when they see others behaving in a particular way. For example, when a website visitor reads testimonials of customers who have had a pleasant experience with your business, they are likely to feel more comfortable doing business with you.

The same applies when a customer tags or mentions your business in their post. When others see the interaction between the customer and your business, it makes you look more credible. Create a call-to-action for customers to leave a review after they have completed their purchase. You can even add an incentive, such as giving them a discount on their next order if they leave a review. In every digital channel, have a designated area for showcasing reviews. For example, you might add them on your website's homepage or as a saved story on Instagram.

4. Create a Google Business profile

You may have noticed that some companies have general business information posted on the first page of Google search results. This offers added convenience to prospective customers, who can simply click on the map and find the location of the business, view their trading hours, or make appointments. If you would also like to have this type of information on the first page of search results, you can create a Google Business profile and add general business information that increases your legitimacy and makes it easier for customers to contact you.

5. Post regularly on social media

You have probably heard about the importance of consistent posting on social media. As a business, you are competing with other similar businesses for the attention of target audience members. The added challenge is that the attention span of social media users has lowered significantly over the years due to the abundance of instant gratification they receive through social media content.

Experts predict that the average user spends a total of eight seconds engaging with content. This means that even if they enjoy your content, they are likely to forget about what they read just a few scrolls later. To stay top-of-mind, you will need to focus on producing interactive or shareable content that gets your audience involved. Examples could include hosting a competition, asking a question, and adding an entertainment factor. Additionally, you will need to post more than once or twice a week to etch your brand in consumers' minds. The recommended number of posts is two to three times per week, and one to two times per day.

BUILDING YOUR ONLINE PRESENCE USING CHATGPT

Being active and consistent is probably one of the best ways to build a sustainable online presence. But let's face it—many business owners simply don't have the time to refresh their websites, create and share compelling posts throughout the week, or keep the conversation going with customers. This is where ChatGPT comes in.

As a business owner, you can use ChatGPT to create different types of online content, ranging from social media copy to blog articles, and everything in between! The chatbot can also assist you with generating call-to-actions and scripts for requesting a review or following up with a customer.

To show you how this works, let's go through a few prompts together! The first type of prompt will help you generate social media captions, specific to the type of platform. Here's an example:

Prompt: Write a social media announcement, using only 200 characters, about a 15% discount on [products or services] over Thanksgiving week-end. Make the announcement relevant to the [social media platform] audience.

Example: Write a social media announcement, using only 200 characters, about a 15% discount on graphic design services over Thanksgiving weekend. Make the announcement relevant to the Instagram audience.

ChatGPT results (OpenAI, 2023):
Give your brand a fresh look this Thanksgiving! Enjoy a mouthwatering 15% OFF on graphic design services all weekend long! Don't miss out, book now! Limited slots available.

#ThanksgivingSpecial #GraphicDesignDiscount #NewLookForYourBrand

As part of the customer purchasing journey, you can create an email requesting a review of the delivered products or services. ChatGPT can help you create the perfect script for the email. Consider the example below:

Prompt: Create an email script, using only 100 words, to request a review from customers, after they have received their product from us. Include details on how they can leave the review. For example, follow the link to our website.

ChatGPT results (OpenAI, 2023):
Subject: We value your feedback! Share your experience with us!

Dear [Customer's Name],
We hope you're enjoying your recent purchase from us! At [Your Company Name], we strive to provide the best possible products and customer service, and your feedback plays a crucial role in helping us achieve that goal.
We kindly request a few minutes of your time to leave a review about your experience with our product. Your honest thoughts will not only help us improve but also assist other customers in making informed decisions.
To leave a review, please visit our website at [Insert Website Link] and navigate to the product page. You'll find an option to share your feedback by clicking on the "Leave a Review" button.
Thank you for being a valued customer. We truly appreciate your support!

Best regards,
[Your Name]
[Your Company Name]

[Your Contact Information]

Another way to use ChatGPT is to ask for suggestions on creating your brand voice. Since you are going to be engaging with customers online, how you speak to them must be consistent with your brand and echo your unique personality. Moreover, having a brand voice helps you stay memorable in the customer's mind, and unconsciously causes them to associate your business with certain values. Below is a prompt that can help you generate a unique brand voice:

Prompt: Create a list of [quantity] qualities, with [quantity] sample phrases, to inform my brand voice. We are a [describe business and offerings]. Keep descriptions short.

> Example: Create a list of one quality, with five sample phrases, to inform my brand voice. We are an online coaching business offering individual and group mentorship services. Keep descriptions short.
>
> ChatGPT results (OpenAI, 2023):
> Quality: Empowering
>
> - Sample phrase 1: "Unlock your potential and discover the power within you."
> - Sample phrase 2: "Embrace your strengths and conquer your goals with our empowering coaching programs."
> - Sample phrase 3: "Ignite your motivation and take charge of your personal growth journey."
> - Sample phrase 4: "Empowering individuals to overcome obstacles and achieve success in all aspects of life."
> - Sample phrase 5: "Experience a transformative coaching experience that empowers you to live a fulfilling and purpose-driven life."

Remember that apart from spreading a lot of information about your business, building an online presence is about establishing meaningful connections with customers and prospective customers. If you are unsure of how to communicate with customers, let ChatGPT help you find your voice!

IN SUMMARY

- It is crucial for businesses that exist exclusively on the internet to have an online presence. Unless you produce content and make prospective customers aware of who you are and how you can help them, they won't be aware of your business.
- Examples of how you can increase your online presence include creating a professional website, creating a blog (if you need one), signing up to the relevant social media platforms, creating a Google Business profile, and posting regularly on social media.
- If you want to save time on producing content for your digital channels, you can seek the assistance of ChatGPT. Not only will the chatbot help you come up with what to say on each platform, but it will also give you guidelines on the best ways to convey the message that are in line with your brand voice.

Now that you understand how to build or increase your online presence, let's cross over to the next chapter and look at how ChatGPT can help you with content marketing.

CHAPTER 14
CREATING YOUR CONTENT MARKETING STRATEGY

Focus on the core problem your business solves and put out lots of content and enthusiasm and ideas about how to solve that problem.

LAURA FITTON

WHAT IS CONTENT MARKETING?

One of the most commonly used strategies to build an online presence is content marketing. This simply refers to the planning, production, and promotion of content that might be of interest to your target audience. Not every type of content will work for your business or appeal to your customers, though, which is why you need to create a content marketing strategy that outlines the various types of content you will produce and share.

Like any other marketing strategy, effective content marketing requires clear goals. Ideally, you want to narrow your options and focus on creating content that helps to achieve specific outcomes. Examples of content marketing goals are:

- to improve brand awareness
- to educate customers on business offerings
- to convert visitors into paying customers
- to boost business revenue
- to improve brand reputation

Note that it is unproductive, as a business, to create content without having a purpose in mind. Every piece of content, whether it is a social media post, blog article, or infographic, should be based on a number of objectives. Through sharing purposeful content, you are able to establish a unique offering to customers and keep them engaged for as long as possible.

TYPES OF CONTENT MARKETING

As mentioned above, not every piece of content will be suitable for your business. For instance, you may find that creating blog articles doesn't help you market your products and services as well as social media posts do. Or perhaps your target audience isn't the type to read email newsletters, so having them wouldn't assist with building strong connections.

If you want to figure out which type of content is appropriate for your business, you should first consider the type of content marketing you want to incorporate into your strategy. Here are a few options:

1. Online content marketing

Online content marketing is the umbrella term to refer to producing and sharing content across the internet, particularly on web pages. Examples of online content marketing include emails, blog articles, banner ads, pay-per-click ads, and social media marketing. To create impactful online marketing content, it is important to leverage keywords that internet users frequently type on search engines like Google. The aim is to ensure that your brand appears on the first few pages of search results.

2. Social media content marketing

Social media content marketing refers to content promotion that occurs on social media platforms only. Each platform will have its own rules and criteria for optimizing content. For example, you may need to pay attention to the size of your photos, length of caption, time of day when you post, and other factors that affect the algorithms. Most social media platforms will offer different types of content to choose from, such as text, photos, audio, long and short-form video, stories, and live streaming. It is up to you to decide how you would like to engage with your target audience.

3. Blog content marketing

Blog content marketing refers to creating shareable content through blog articles. Your content could be as simple as writing about a topic customers would be interested in, or incorporating links to your products or affiliate websites to encourage them to make a purchase. SEO-optimized content is important to ensure that your article appears on the first few pages of search results.

4. Infographic content marketing

Did you know that around 60% of businesses incorporate infographics into their content strategy (Woodward, 2023)? It may not be one of the more widely spoken about types of content marketing, but it is effective for conveying data in an easy-to-understand manner. Since social media users spend only a few seconds on a post, presenting information in a visually appealing way can increase your post engagement. Some businesses go a step further and find ways of repurposing infographics by transforming them into animated educational videos or tutorials. In this way, the same information can be shared creatively, using different media forms.

5. Paid ads content marketing

Paid ads content marketing refers to putting money behind content to increase its reach and engagement. Many digital channels offer paid ads content marketing. The most popular channel for this type of marketing is social media; however, you can also create ads for your website, Google search pages, and email marketing.

CREATING A CONTENT MARKETING STRATEGY USING CHATGPT

A content marketing strategy explains the various ways you will reach and engage with your target audience using different types of content. At the core of your strategy are specific goals that you want to achieve through online marketing. These goals inform your digital channel selection, as well as the different content forms you will utilize. After you have created your strategy, all that's left to do is content creation!

ChatGPT is a great tool to use when you are creating a content marketing strategy. Not only can the chatbot generate a detailed plan for you, but it can also help you choose the best online platforms and types of content to showcase your business. The hardest part is finding the right prompts to get the process started. But don't panic, below are a few prompts to get you inspired!

The first prompt helps you identify the most suitable online channels to incorporate into your strategy. Remember, you only want to showcase your business on channels that your target audience frequently visits or engages with. Consider the following prompt:

Prompt: Which digital channels are the best for connecting with [describe target audience]? Rank them, without providing a description.

> Example: Which digital channels are the best for connecting with suburban mothers between the ages of 40 and 60, who are planning for retirement? Rank them, without providing a description.

ChatGPT results (OpenAI, 2023):

1. Facebook
2. Email newsletters
3. LinkedIn
4. YouTube
5. Pinterest
6. Instagram
7. Twitter
8. TikTok

Once you have selected your list of digital channels, you can create a smaller plan for each channel. Every plan should start with meaningful content goals that are appropriate for that specific channel. For example, what works for social media marketing may not be appropriate for email marketing. Therefore, your prompt should help you create specific goals for each channel. Here is an example:

Prompt: I am using [specify digital channel] to connect with [specify target audience]. List content goals to focus on.

Example: I am using email marketing to connect with suburban mothers between the ages of 40 and 60. List content goals to focus on.

ChatGPT results (OpenAI, 2023):
When using email marketing to connect with suburban mothers between the ages of 40 and 60 who are planning for retirement, you can focus on the following content goals:

1. Retirement planning tips and strategies
2. Financial advice for saving and investing for retirement
3. Health and wellness tips for a happy and active retirement
4. Ideas for hobbies, travel, and leisure activities in retirement

5. Stories and testimonials from other women in similar situations
6. Information on healthcare and insurance options for retirement
7. Resources for continuing education or pursuing new career paths in retirement
8. Advice on downsizing, decluttering, and organizing for a simplified retirement lifestyle
9. Supportive and motivational content to help mothers navigate the emotional aspects of retirement planning
10. Updates on relevant events, workshops, and webinars related to retirement planning.

Remember to personalize your emails, use engaging subject lines, and include compelling calls to action to encourage interaction and response from your target audience.

Lastly, you can ask ChatGPT to recommend the best media form to share your content, specific to the preferences of your target audience. Here is a prompt you can try:

Prompt: Based on the preferences of [specify target audience], what are the best media forms to share content? Provide a list with examples of type of content.

Example: Based on the preferences of suburban mothers between the ages of 40 and 60 who are planning for retirement, what are the best media forms to share content? Provide a list with examples of type of content.

ChatGPT results (OpenAI, 2023):
Based on the preferences of suburban mothers between the ages of 40 and 60 who are planning for retirement, here are some of the best media forms to share content, along with examples of the types of content that can be shared:
The best media forms to share content with suburban mothers

between the ages of 40 and 60 who are planning for retirement can include a mix of digital and traditional channels. Here's a list of media forms along with examples of the type of content for each:

1. Email Newsletters:

- Retirement planning tips and strategies
- Financial advice and investment guides
- Inspirational stories of successful retirees
- Health and wellness tips for seniors

2. Blogs and Articles:

- Comprehensive retirement guides and checklists
- Expert interviews and insights on retirement planning
- Personal anecdotes and experiences of other women in retirement
- Retirement destination spotlights and travel ideas

3. Webinars and Video Content:

- Live or recorded webinars on retirement topics
- Video interviews with financial advisors and retirement experts
- Virtual tours of retirement communities or travel destinations
- Exercise and fitness routines for seniors

4. Social Media:

- Facebook: Community discussions on retirement planning
- Instagram: Inspirational quotes and retirement lifestyle images
- LinkedIn: Professional networking and career transition advice
- Pinterest: Visual boards with retirement ideas and DIY projects

5. Podcasts:

- Retirement success stories and lessons learned
- Expert-hosted episodes on financial planning and investment strategies
- Conversations about health, mental well-being, and staying active in retirement
- Discussions on transitioning from full-time work to retirement.

The major advantage of using ChatGPT to create a content marketing strategy is that it can help you tailor your plan to address the specific needs of your target audience. Say goodbye to guessing what customers need because now you will be able to create content that appeals to their wants and needs.

IN SUMMARY

- A content marketing strategy is one of the ways to build an online presence. It is based on researching, designing, and sharing content that increases engagement with your target audience.
- Every content marketing strategy is founded on a goal, such as building awareness, increasing revenue, or converting followers into paying customers. Having a goal allows you to focus on producing specific types of content that get your target audience to take action.
- ChatGPT is a useful tool to use when drafting your content marketing strategy. It is capable of sourcing tailored data that considers the needs, interests, and preferences of your specific target audience.

Now that you understand how to create a content marketing strategy, let's cross over to the next chapter and look at how ChatGPT can help you with customer service.

CHAPTER 15
ENHANCE YOUR CUSTOMER SERVICE EXPERIENCE

Customer service is just a day-in, day-out, ongoing, never-ending, unremitting, persevering, compassionate type of activity.

LEON GORMAN

WHAT IS CUSTOMER SERVICE?

It is expected that customers will reach out to you whenever they need more information about your products or services, run into an issue transacting, or have concerns to discuss with you. The business department that manages customer relations and communication is known as customer service. For traditional businesses, it may simply be called "customer service," but since you have an online business, your relationships with customers will be built and nurtured through virtual support.

Customer service can be defined as the process of assisting customers with their needs, queries, and complaints through digital channels. At times, it may also involve solving different kinds of problems that customers may have. You can choose the best ways for customers to reach you, such as via telephone, email, social media messaging, business apps, website chatbots, or website contact forms. In general, the more options you make available for customers, the more convenient you make the process for them.

WHY IS CUSTOMER SERVICE IMPORTANT?

Have you ever experienced poor customer service, such as struggling to get through to a business, or when you finally do, talking to someone who lacks empathy or doesn't know how to assist you? After the long waiting times, unprofessional support, and unsuccessful attempt at solving your problem, you made a vow to never do business with that company again. *Am I right?*

Now, think about a time when you experienced exceptional customer service. It may have happened on a few occasions. When you visited the website or messaged the business on social media, you were greeted by a chatbot that was programmed to assist you with frequently asked questions. Within five minutes you received the help you needed, and an hour later, you received an email from a customer service team representative, asking if there was anything else you needed.

How did you feel after receiving such good service? Did you feel valued by the business? The exchange was rehearsed, professional, and pleasant, providing you with the knowledge or support you were looking for. If you weren't already thinking of making another purchase, you certainly planned on doing business with the company again in the near future.

Customers are human first, which means that when they engage with your business, they expect to be treated with a certain level of respect and empathy. Think about how you would respond to a friend's phone call or address an older family member. Your customers are no different from a friend, family member, or colleague. Above and beyond getting the assistance they are looking for, customers want to be validated and to feel as though their needs matter to you. Bringing that human touch to sales is what makes customers feel seen and valued.

Great online customer service focuses on establishing that human touch. This is extremely important for an online business that will probably never get the opportunity to physically interact with customers. The bond between you and your customers rests on your level of responsiveness and communication. When you respond immediately to customer queries, they feel like a priority. And when you communicate with respect and empathy, they feel validated.

HOW TO PROVIDE GREAT CUSTOMER SERVICE

Statistics show that over half of customers (53%) will abandon their purchase online if they can't quickly solve their problem. The reason for having such little patience is that they know that the same product or service can be purchased on another online store, without going through all of the hassle.

Having outstanding customer service can be the make-or-break factor for your business, allowing you to poach customers from fellow competitors. Your focus should be on providing a seamless process that anticipates customers' needs and limits the time it takes for them to make a purchase decision.

If you are looking for strategies to improve customer service for your online business, here are some to consider:

- **Offer customers self-service resources.** You may be an online business, but there will be times when you are unavailable via phone or email. Creating self-service resources ensures that customers are supported around the clock. Present the resources in different formats (i.e. articles, videos, tutorials, etc.) to cater to as many customer preferences as you can.

- **Present multiple options to contact you.** Since your business is online, calling in may not be a viable option for every customer— particularly those who live overseas. Your contact methods should seek to accommodate as many customers as possible and be visible enough for customers to see on each channel. For example, you can add contact information on a web page, social media bio, email signature, or on a live chat.

- **Create groups where customers can help each other.** A sustainable way to manage online customer service is to create a space where customers can congregate and share tips, advice, and knowledge. This community-like group can be built on a mobile app like WhatsApp, online forums, or social media platforms. After a new customer makes their first purchase, you can send them a link to the group, where they will find other like-minded people. To keep them engaged in the group, consider running promotions, competitions, or starting a loyalty program.

- **Personalize the customer service experience.** Mentioning your customer's name in an email is only one way of personalizing communication. Other ways include triggering automated notification messages whenever your customers take a certain action on your website, sending an email when they haven't visited your website in a while, or learning their preferences and sending them emails with custom offers.

- **Consider using ticket software.** If you are running a service business, such as building websites, you may have customers reaching out frequently to ask questions or present issues with their service. Since many of these issues will require troubleshooting, which takes a lot of back-and-forth testing, you can use a ticket system to get customers to wait in a queue, keep track of who you have helped, categorize some tickets as priority tasks, and view a history of conversations or specific issues that have been brought up in the past.

The more customers you do business with, the more time and effort you will need to invest in your customer service. What's common among both satisfied and unsatisfied customers is that they do a lot of talking! If you aren't careful, you can earn a bad reputation among prospective customers due to the dissatisfaction of a few.

ELEVATING YOUR CUSTOMER SERVICE WITH CHATGPT

AI tools like chatbots have been around since the late 1960s. The concept of a machine imitating a real human-like conversation is not new and certainly didn't start with ChatGPT. However, what makes ChatGPT stand out from other AI chatbots is that it can troubleshoot, pick up on sentiments and offer advice, anticipate customer needs, and personalize communication for different customer personas. Nevertheless, without creating quality prompts, you won't be able to get the best out of this one-of-a-kind chatbot.

Below are some useful prompts to help you elevate your customer service. The first prompt asks ChatGPT to solve an issue that a customer is having while transacting on an online store:

Prompt: Here is my customer's problem: [explain the issue]. Please help me solve the problem by offering three possible solutions.

Example: Here is my customer's problem: Customer is trying to add items in her shopping cart but the items won't reflect. Shopping cart is empty despite her attempts. Please help me solve the problem by offering three possible solutions.

ChatGPT results (OpenAI, 2023):
I'm sorry to hear about the issue your customer is experiencing with adding items to her shopping cart. Here are three possible solutions to help resolve the problem:

1. Clear the browser cache and cookies: Sometimes, stored data can cause conflicts and prevent items from being added to the shopping cart. Ask the customer to clear their browser cache and cookies and then try adding items again. They can usually do this by going to the browser settings or preferences and selecting the option to clear browsing data.
2. Disable browser extensions: Certain browser extensions or add-ons can interfere with website functionality, including the shopping cart. Ask the customer to temporarily disable any extensions they have installed, particularly those related to ad-blocking or privacy, and then try adding items to the cart again.
3. Try a different browser or device: It's possible that the issue is specific to the browser or device being used. Ask the customer to try accessing the website and adding items to the cart using a different browser (e.g. Chrome, Firefox, Safari) or a different device (e.g. smartphone, tablet). This can help determine if the problem is isolated to a particular environment.

If none of these solutions resolve the issue, it may be necessary to gather more specific information about the problem, such as the browser and operating system versions being used, any error messages displayed, or any recent changes made to the website. This additional information can help further troubleshoot and diagnose the problem.

ChatGPT is also intelligent enough to pick up on customer sentiments and offer advice on how to respond to them. For example, if your customer left a review online and you aren't sure how to respond in the right manner, you can share the review with ChatGPT and the chatbot can provide appropriate feedback. Consider the following example:

Prompt: My customer left the following review online: [copy the review]. Provide a 50-word empathetic script.

Example: My customer left the following review online: "I am underwhelmed about my recent experience working with Sam. I asked her to write a few SEO articles for my blog. While she is pleasant to work with, I find her time management questionable." Provide a 50-word empathetic script.

ChatGPT results (OpenAI, 2023):
Dear valued customer,
Thank you for sharing your feedback about your recent experience with Sam. We sincerely apologize for any inconvenience caused. We understand the importance of timely delivery and will address the issue with Sam to ensure better time management in the future. We appreciate your patience and would be happy to make it right.

You never have to face customers alone when you have ChatGPT. Whatever customer-related problem you may have, the chatbot can help you resolve it, pronto!

IN SUMMARY

- Customer service is the process of responding to customer needs, queries, and complaints using various channels. The aim is to reduce as many barriers to contacting the business so that customers are helped in the shortest time possible.
- Online businesses rely heavily on customer service to build and nurture relationships with their customers. For some businesses, offering exceptional customer service is what gives them a competitive edge.
- There are different strategies that can improve your online customer service, such as offering self-service resources, multiple contact methods, and personalization communication.

Fortunately, ChatGPT can assist you with many customer-related tasks, so you don't have to manage customers on your own!

Now that you understand how to enhance your customer service, let's cross over to Part 6 and look at how ChatGPT can help you kickstart your freelancing career!

PART SIX
FREELANCING WITH CHATGPT

CHAPTER 16
THE BASICS OF FREELANCING

If you are not willing to risk the unusual, you will have to settle for the ordinary.

JIM ROHN

WHAT IS FREELANCING?

When you think of remote jobs, you may think of freelancing. However, this trillion-dollar industry has a lot more perks than just working from home. Statistics show that 84% of full-time freelancers report having the freedom to live the lifestyle they want, and 64% said that their health drastically improved after switching careers (Djuraskovic, 2021).

So, what exactly is freelancing, and how can you get involved?

We can define freelancing as contractual work performed for a number of clients. Freelancers typically sell their skills or knowledge in exchange for money. Instead of being paid at the end of the month, they are paid after each successful project. Similar to an entrepreneur who promotes their business, freelancers will need to advertise their services in order to bring in new clients and provide unique value to existing clients.

The majority of freelancing takes place on designated freelancing market-places, where freelancers create accounts and market their services to people looking for assistance with various creative, financial, technical, or administrative tasks. Apart from these marketplaces, some freelancers expand their reach by creating personal blogs and social media accounts to showcase their portfolio of work.

Many successful freelancers are able to turn their craft into a full-time career. The law classifies them as self-employed, and they are required to pay the same taxes as sole traders. Similar to entrepreneurs, they get to set their own hours, cost of labor, and how many tasks or projects they will accept at a time. However, as flexible and lucrative as freelancing can be, it does come with a few drawbacks.

PROS AND CONS OF FREELANCING

Before you go headfirst into freelancing, it is important to understand what you are getting yourself into. For instance, if you are transitioning from a traditional 9-to-5 to freelancing, there may be a few adjustments you need to make. Below are a few pros and cons of freelancing to give you an idea of what your journey may look like:

Let's start with some pros:

- **You can work from anywhere.** You will notice that most of your freelancing gigs are sourced and completed online, which means that you can work for clients in different parts of the country or the world without traveling to their offices. You also get to set work hours and how many projects to take on.
- **You choose what type of work to do.** Unlike traditional 9-to-5s where you are assigned duties and may be limited when it comes to your scope of work, you get to choose which industries you want to service, what set of tasks you want to specialize in, and the complexity of projects you are willing to take on.

- **You get the opportunity to set your own rates.** Freelancers are usually paid per hour, but have flexibility when it comes to setting their rates. Of course, your rates should be competitive in order to attract clients. However, you could potentially earn more per hour as a freelancer than you would by working a traditional job.

The benefits of freelancing are great, but what's the catch? Here are a few cons of being a freelancer:

- **You may struggle to get a good work-life balance.** Since you get to work from home and set your own hours, it is very easy to blur the lines between work hours and personal hours. If you are unable to set boundaries for yourself, freelancing can end up consuming a lot of time, causing you to work more than you rest.
- **You don't get any employee benefits.** Freelancing doesn't come with traditional benefits like medical cover, unemployment insurance, sick leave, vacation leave, and a pension fund. It is also difficult to take time off as a freelancer because the money you earn sustains your livelihood. If you stop working, there won't be any money coming in.
- **You face a lot of job uncertainty.** There is no such thing as a fixed or permanent job for a freelancer. As soon as the contract is over, you need to look for more work. If you are lucky, you may be able to partner with a company and provide your services for a 6 or 12-month contract. During that period, you are paid a retainer on a month-to-month basis. However, generally speaking, many freelance gigs last for a few hours up to a few weeks.

Having learned about the downside of freelancing, are you still motivated to make a career (or side hustle) out of it?

BEST FREELANCING PLATFORMS

Earlier in the book, we spoke about the startup capital required to start a business. Even though freelancers are treated like entrepreneurs, they don't need to have startup capital to start making money. Registering an account on freelancing marketplaces is free. Plus, you get the chance to build a customer base without having to spend money looking for them on your own.

Below is a list of popular freelancing platforms that help you promote your skills and find clients:

- **Toptal:** This platform caters to freelancers who have already built a portfolio of work and are one of the best in their various industries. The selection criteria to get accepted are high because they only want to attract the best talent for some of their clients, like Microsoft and Salesforce. So, even though it is difficult to get in, you can make a lot of money if you are accepted.
- **Guru:** This platform is among the largest freelancing sites on the internet. It is a great place to learn how to build your freelancing business because it offers a variety of pricing strategies to choose from. The only downside is that the site takes a fee from your invoice after you get paid.
- **Upwork:** This is perhaps one of the most popular platforms that mostly attracts freelancers in the fields of marketing and software, however, you can find other types of work represented too. It is suitable for freelancers looking for medium to long-term contracts, and who aren't afraid of taking on challenges, such as creating strategies or solving complex problems for businesses. The site will take a fee from every completed job but charges less on larger projects.
- **99Designs:** This platform was specifically created for freelancers offering design and branding services. For example, if you are able to design logos, book covers, or websites, this site is suitable

for you. The site allows you to promote your creative services like other platforms. It also hosts contests created by clients that freelancers can join by submitting designs. Clients choose the best designs and pay the winning freelancers for their designs. Like many other freelancing platforms, 99Designs charges a once-off fee after your first gig, and a fee after every completed work.

- **Fiverr:** Another great platform for newbies is Fiverr. It has a large database of freelancers and claims to bring a traffic of 4.3 million clients each year (Woodward, 2023). Since this site is so big, you are able to specialize and offer niche services that clients wouldn't be able to find elsewhere. Joining and posting listings is free, however, the transaction fees tend to be higher compared to other sites.

Bear in mind that these are only five out of hundreds of freelancing sites online. No matter what skills or knowledge you have to share, you are guaranteed to find a platform that attracts clients looking for freelancers just like you!

IN SUMMARY

- Freelancing is contractual work entered into by a freelancer and a client. In exchange for money, the freelancer offers their skills and knowledge. The relationship between the parties lasts as long as the contract stipulates. Thereafter, the freelancer must look for more work.
- There are many benefits to freelancing, such as the ability to set your own rates, hours, and workload. You can also decide what type of work you want to do, and what type of contracts you prefer.
- Unlike entrepreneurs, there are low barriers to entry to become a freelancer. For example, you don't need to have startup capital or

a business plan to start making money. You can simply sign up on a freelancing platform and build a customer base from there.

Now that you understand what it means to be a freelancer, let's cross over to the next chapter and look at how you can start a freelancing business.

CHAPTER 17
STARTING YOUR
FREELANCE BUSINESS

Pleasure in the job puts perfection in the work.

ARISTOTLE

IS IT THE BEST TIME TO START YOUR OWN FREELANCE BUSINESS?

When ChatGPT was first released, there were mixed feelings about its impact on the world of work. Professionals in the creative industries had fears (and some still do) that generative AI tools like ChatGPT would replace their jobs. For instance, due to the automation of tasks like writing, authors and copywriters were worried that their services wouldn't be needed anymore. While these fears are valid, they are not necessarily true—at least for now, since there is still decades of time before AI tools are able to replace human beings at work.

About 33% of jobs in the creative industries are freelance jobs (Thrasyvoulou, 2023). This number is growing by the day, as contract jobs (rather than full-time jobs) experience a greater demand. Companies are realizing that they can get more value for money when they work with highly skilled contractors for the duration of projects, instead of employing professionals full-time and not having access to a greater pool of skills and knowledge.

You might have noticed the shift from full-time to contract work, and desire to start freelancing, but fear that one day you will be replaced by a chatbot. Even though chatbots like ChatGPT are built on artificial intelligence, they don't have human intelligence. This means that rather than competing with chatbots, there is an opportunity for you to partner with chatbots to make your freelancing career more dynamic.

Here are a few reasons why freelancers shouldn't have to worry about being replaced by AI:

- **AI chatbots lack creativity.** The results you are able to generate from chatbots like ChatGPT are not unique. If you took the time to search the internet, you would find similar thoughts. However, a creative person is capable of using their imagination and experience to produce compelling insights and solve unique problems that have not yet been explored on the internet.
- **AI chatbots produce generic content.** The appeal of ChatGPT is that it is capable of combining your ideas and producing results that are relevant and sometimes accurate. Nevertheless, these results are standard for anybody who might use the same prompts. The risk of duplication, poor quality assurance, and plagiarism are still major disadvantages of relying on AI chatbots.
- **AI chatbots lack human judgment.** One of the reasons why companies pay for the services of creative people is that they are intuitive and score high in emotional intelligence. The insights, arguments, and innovative solutions they can come up with are of a higher standard than an AI chatbot. Creative people are also great at discerning subtleties in text, such as how certain words or phrases might be perceived by readers. This is something that ChatGPT may not always get right.

- **AI chatbots have knowledge, but limited experiences.** Creative people outperform chatbots due to one factor—experience. Some creative people don't even need to be "taught" to think creatively; it is an innate gift they were born with. ChatGPT is taught how to think and interpret information. As such, it is unable to adapt to situations that are not predetermined. For instance, on some prompts, the chatbot will state that it doesn't have the knowledge to answer the question.

If you still have doubts about whether you will be replaced by an AI chatbot one day, take a look at ChatGPT's response when asked to answer this very question:

Prompt: Be honest ChatGPT, will you replace my job as a freelance writer one day?

ChatGPT results (OpenAI, 2023):
As an AI language model, I can understand why you might have concerns about the potential impact of AI on various job roles, including freelance writing. While AI technology has made significant advancements in generating written content, it is important to note that AI like myself are still tools designed to assist and enhance human capabilities, rather than outright replace them. As of now, AI language models like ChatGPT are most effective when working in collaboration with human writers. We can provide suggestions, generate ideas, or even draft sections of text, but the final decisions and creative elements are best handled by human writers who bring their unique perspectives and insights to the table.

HOW TO START YOUR FREELANCE BUSINESS

If you are planning to freelance full-time, you may be interested in starting a freelance business or agency. The business model for a freelance business is simple: You are the sole employer and employee. The services you offer are the skills you are great at. Everything else, in terms of sales and markets, works similarly to a normal online business.

When starting a freelance agency, the business model changes slightly. Instead of being the sole employee whose skills keep the business going, you create an online platform and invite multiple freelancers to join and bid for work. Like any other online business, you will need to market your platform to attract paying clients, so that freelancers are able to get consistent work coming in. But the difference is that you stand to make greater profits through commissions charged after each successful project facilitated by you.

Whether you are leaning toward a traditional freelance business or starting your own agency, it can be good practice to spend a year as a full-time freelancer and learn the tricks of the trade. Gaining firsthand experience as a freelancer can help you conduct field research and identify specific market gaps that your agency can close. If you are considering going this route, here are a few steps to start your own freelance business:

1. Identify skills you can turn into business services

It is rare for freelancers to sell physical products. In most cases, they offer skills or knowledge-sharing as services. The best way to compete in the freelancing industry is to capitalize on what you are good at.

Of course, the closer you are to the mastery level, the better. However, you can start out as an amateur and gain experience in your craft. More important than being an expert in what you do is being passionate about it. Passion is contagious, and usually jumps out of a screen and infects the person who is reading your profile or perusing through your work.

Similar to online businesses, offering a niche service will help you stand out. This means that regardless of the skill you plan on offering, ensure you present it in a unique way. For example, instead of just being a ghostwriter, you can also offer editing and proofreading services to save clients time and money working with multiple freelancers on a single project.

Over time, you can also strive toward specializing in your craft, such as offering ghostwriting services for children's books only. This is another way of differentiating yourself from competitors.

2. Put together your marketing strategy

If you aren't going to join a freelance platform, you will need to have a plan for how to market your services and attract the right target audience. This process is no different than an online business marketing itself online. For example, you would need to complete a digital channel selection, create a goal for each channel, and figure out the best content to share to drive engagement. Since your services are creative, you can go wild thinking of unique ways to promote your services.

For example, if your business niche is teaching aspiring content writers how to become ghostwriters, you may decide to write a book or online course about ghostwriting and share your digital products on e-learning sites, your business website, and social media. Those who purchase your book or course may receive a discount for individual or group coaching sessions. You may even decide to start a podcast and explain the process and experience of ghostwriting in each podcast episode. Don't forget to consult with ChatGPT when compiling your marketing strategy!

3. Put together a pricing strategy

Another important component of your business is pricing. Like any other business, the aim is to generate revenue, so you shouldn't price your services too low. Many freelancers opt to price per hour instead of a once-off payment for a project because they take into consideration the time and energy required to think creatively. Freelancers who have more than two years of experience may even charge a premium due to their expertise.

It is important to find a pricing strategy that works for you and ensures that you are adequately compensated for your skills and time. As part of your market research, find out the average rates of freelancers within your field to get an idea of your starting point.

4. Check the legal requirements

In the eyes of US law, freelancers are seen as sole proprietors—whether they establish a business or not. Therefore, it is crucial to read up on the laws about sole proprietorships, such as when and how to pay taxes, and how much liability protection they have. These laws will all apply to you. For example, your default business name will be your full legal name (unless you register a "doing business as" name). You are also not mandated to open a business bank account, since you are not seen as a separate entity from your business.

5. Network, network, network

The sustainability of your freelance business depends on the number of recurring clients you serve. Networking is the process of building and nurturing relationships with your peers, potential clients, and industry associations. As a freelancer, you never know where your next business will come from. For instance, due to your relationship with industry associations, you may be approached by companies that are looking for contractors. Or maybe due to your relationship with freelancers in other industries, you may be approached by one of your peers to collaborate on a project that requires your skills.

Being effective at networking is about understanding who you are and what you have to offer others. Instead of focusing on what you can get, pay attention to the value you provide. Remember, people prefer to do business with people they like. The best way to be likable is to have some unique value you offer others, for free. Some of the ways to share your value include creating monthly newsletters, providing free consultations, launching a referral program, and volunteering your services to a local nonprofit organization.

Starting a freelance business doesn't require as much work as a traditional online business. However, since you are the sole employer and employee, a lot rides on your ability to provide labor and manage your business at the same time. Nevertheless, you still have the flexibility to determine work hours, cost of labor, and how many projects you take on.

IN SUMMARY

- Now is the best time to become a freelancer due to the growing demand for contractors in the global workforce. Companies are starting to realize they can get more value for money when they outsource niche services.
- There is no reason to fear that you will be replaced by an AI chatbot one day. Tools like ChatGPT have been created to complement your work as a creative person, not compete with it. Plus, there are many advantages you have over chatbots, such as intuition, experience, and discernment.
- Starting a freelance business looks similar to starting an online business. The only difference is that you are both the employer and the employee. You will still need to market your services using the same strategies as online businesses, and the law treats you the same as a sole proprietor and will thus expect you to follow those regulations.

Now that you understand what it takes to start your freelance business, let's cross over to the next chapter and look at ways to be competitive, negotiate your rates, and manage multiple projects.

CHAPTER 18
SETTING YOURSELF UP FOR SUCCESS AS A FREELANCER

Look up at the stars and not down at your feet. Try to make sense of what you see, and wonder about what makes the universe exist. Be curious.

STEPHEN HAWKING

WHAT GIVES FREELANCERS THE COMPETITIVE EDGE?

We have spoken about what gives online businesses a competitive edge. But what about freelancers? How do they compete?

One thing is for sure: Freelancing is not easy. Even though starting out requires very little investment, making money takes a lot of effort. The major issue that freelancers face is getting consistent work. For instance, on sites like Upwork which have over 12 million registered freelancers, you won't get every job that you apply for. Plus, as if you needed any more competition, you also need to find a way to make your skills somehow more "saleable" than the next freelancer.

So, how can you compete in such a saturated industry where the competition is so high? The simple answer is finding a competitive edge. The best way to describe a competitive edge is a quality or experience that makes you stand out. It isn't so much something physical that you can put in a box, but rather something that clients feel when they do business with you.

Your competitive edge as a freelancer could be your infectious personality that causes clients to seek your services, even when there is another freelancer who offers cheaper services. They want to do business with you because of how you make them feel.

Another example of a competitive edge is your talent; those abilities you were born with. It is important to differentiate between talent and skills since these concepts can be confused with each other. Skills are tools that you are trained to become an expert in using. It typically takes years to learn how to use the tools proficiently. After intense training, you can charge clients money to utilize your skills.

Talent, on the other hand, is an unearned advantage that you are given from birth. Sometimes, you cannot explain why you are so good at your talent, even though you didn't go to school for it. The reason why your talent gives you a competitive edge is because, unlike skills, it is difficult to imitate someone else's talent.

For example, everybody is capable of learning painting techniques and calling themselves an artist. However, there is only one Pablo Picasso to have ever lived. Similarly, anyone can learn the craft of writing books, and call themselves an author, but there is only one J. K. Rowling.

Your competitive edge could also be in the way you conduct business. For instance, you might have a unique process that you take clients through that has been proven to be efficient. Clients may enjoy working with you because you make their projects run smoother, or keep the communication flowing.

Competing as a freelancer is about leveraging these unique abilities or advantages that nobody besides you can offer. If you struggle to identify these unique abilities and advantages, perhaps you can take a free personality assessment online and get to know more about what makes you special!

STRATEGIES TO GET MORE CLIENTS

On a practical level, you will need to actively go out of your way to find clients, and keep them coming back to you.

If sales and marketing are not your personal strength, don't worry. You can build an online presence by following these tips:

- **Create a social media page:** You can find clients across the internet, including social media. However, in order for people to take your craft seriously, consider creating a page exclusively for promoting your work. Create content, curated for each platform, that you believe your target audience would engage with.
- **Join industry groups:** One of the best ways to get to meet potential clients is to go where they are. If your target audience is companies looking to hire freelancers, then you can consider joining spaces or groups where professionals congregate.
- **Share your thoughts:** Your meaningful contribution in the form of thought leadership posts on social media or helpful comments on forums can get people to notice you. Remind yourself that your skills are in demand, and the best way to market them is by sharing your thoughts about related topics and offering free advice.
- **Create a portfolio of work:** As a freelancer, you are the face of your business. Thus, before clients agree to do business with you, they will want to know more about your expertise. Besides obtaining the necessary qualifications, think of ways to demonstrate your skills and knowledge in creative ways. For instance, you might create a course, send out a free monthly newsletter, or write a book sharing your skills with others.

- **Send requests to become a guest contributor on websites:**
  Another way to get your name and business out there is to
  become a guest contributor on reputable websites that your
  target audience may subscribe to. In most cases, you will need to
  send a proposal or sample of work to the website admins to find
  out if you can publish articles or creative work on their platforms.
  Depending on which sites your target audience frequently visits,
  you can reach out to blogs, online magazines, or even established
  podcasts.

Whenever you are looking for creative ways to promote yourself as a
freelancer, it can be helpful to think of yourself as a brand. For instance, if
you were a marketing manager, how would you present yourself as a
brand to audiences? Which digital channels would be most suitable for
your brand? What type of content would your target audience expect
from you? These questions can help you think of innovative ways to
showcase your skills online.

IT'S TIME FOR NEGOTIATIONS

Your rates as a freelancer aren't set in stone. This is a good thing because
it means that you can set seasonal rates, rates per project, rates per hour,
or rates per task. Moreover, the fact that your rates aren't fixed means you
can work with each client to come up with a price that is comfortable for
both of you.

Many freelancers are afraid to ask for what they are worth. They would
rather settle for how much the client can afford. Furthermore, since they
are aware that there is stiff competition for gigs, they are more likely to
agree on being paid under their minimum rate than negotiating for a
higher rate.

In order to enjoy freelancing, you must feel like it is worth the time and
effort you invest in producing quality work. If you don't cut corners

when doing the work, you shouldn't cut corners when you are asking to be compensated fairly.

To make negotiations less awkward for you, consider practicing these tips the next time you discuss rates with clients:

1. Compare your hourly rates to what someone working in corporate would charge

As a freelancer, you are supposed to be paid according to your skill level. While you may not be in the corporate space, the same salary pay ranges apply to you. Think about the title you would be given if you worked at a corporation and find the average hourly rate for that position. You may choose to make that rate your minimum, or simply use it as an argument to justify your freelance rate. The best sites to find industry average earnings are Glassdoor, PayScale, and Indeed Salary Explorer.

2. Set rate nonnegotiables

Something that you can think about when you are on your own are freelance rate nonnegotiables. These are the boundaries you set to protect you from undercutting yourself. For example, you might enforce a rule that your minimum rate must at least cover your monthly expenses, or that your rate for complex projects must take into consideration the time spent researching and problem-solving. When you enter negotiations with certain boundaries established, it is easier to turn down rates that don't fit your criteria.

3. Upsell your services

Upselling is a sales technique to get more revenue from a customer by suggesting add-ons or upgrades to their service. The customer ends up getting more value for their money, and the seller gets to charge more for each purchase. As a freelancer, you can upsell your services by creating valuable add-ons. For example, if you are selling copywriting services, you can add editing and proofreading as an add-on, and increase your rate. The aim is to offer value for money, so make sure that your add-ons are services your clients actually need.

4. Put yourself in your client's shoes

Your freelance rates should be mindful of your client's needs and any constraints they might have. For instance, if you are offering services to a newly-formed startup, they may not have a lot of cash to put toward certain tasks. By understanding their position, you can find ways of accommodating them without necessarily selling yourself short. You might decide to give startup business owners a special discount on services to help them manage costs.

5. Know when to walk away from the table

It is unfortunate but true that many freelancers are exploited for their labor due to there being so much competition for work. It is important to understand how much your services are worth before entering any bids. When clients are going below your minimum rate, know when to compromise and when to simply walk away from the table. Yes, this could mean losing a potential lifetime client, but at least you get to preserve your dignity. Have your nonnegotiable in check and be comfortable saying "That won't work for me!"

HOW TO MANAGE PROJECTS AS A FREELANCER

When you manage to find the right marketing mix and pricing strategy, you will have clients flocking to your page or website. The good news is that you have a lot of work, but the bad news is that you will need to find ways to manage the increasing workload.

If you are a one-man or one-woman team, then you will be responsible for completing 100% of the projects. Effective time management will be vital to stay on track with your deadlines and give each project the time and dedication it needs. Below are a few time management tips to help you manage multiple projects:

- **Give yourself a reasonable amount of time:** You may be tempted to impress clients by delivering fast results, but depending on the demands of the project, this may not be possible. Be realistic about how long a project will take you, and factor in days of rest to take care of yourself.
- **Hold yourself accountable:** Create systems to hold yourself accountable for the progress you are making. For example, you can set daily and weekly targets, then assess how often you are meeting those targets. It is also important to set clear work and personal boundaries to train your mind when to focus and switch off.
- **Keep clients informed:** Another way to hold yourself accountable is to frequently check in with clients and update them on your progress. This will also put their minds at ease, knowing that the project is going according to plan.
- **Practice single-tasking:** Train your mind to give full attention to a single task, until you have completed it. Block out time on your calendar to avoid using that time for anything else besides your single task. Reward yourself after every successful attempt at single-tasking.
- **Start with the difficult tasks:** You may be someone who postpones difficult tasks, thinking they will take up a lot of your time. However, the longer you postpone them, the more overwhelmed you will feel. Starting your day or week with the most difficult tasks can change your perspective on them. Even if they do end up becoming challenging, your willingness to prioritize the task can help you stay open-minded and motivated to solve the problems.

- **Write everything down:** Writing things down can reduce overthinking and improve your organizational skills. Checklists are good for writing down your daily tasks and reminders or scribbling down spontaneous ideas that come to your mind.

Running a freelance business on your own requires careful planning and time management. This is why it can be a game changer to take advantage of technology tools. Thankfully, there are many apps and software, like Asana, Trello, and Planzer.io that can help you schedule meetings, sync your calendars, manage client projects and tasks, and track the progress of each project. You can also use ChatGPT to create schedules and routines, and track how well you are maximizing your time.

IN SUMMARY

- There's no doubt that the freelance business isn't a walk in the park. The competition is stiff, and the only way to get noticed is to find ways of standing out from the rest. In most cases, this means finding your competitive edge; that quality or experience that nobody else can replicate.
- Like online businesses, you will need to create a marketing strategy to promote your freelance business. If this sounds daunting to you, imagine that you are a brand and your clients are members of your target audience. Draft a strategy that would showcase your brand in the best light.
- Time is a valuable commodity for you as a freelancer; however, it can either work for or against you. For instance, you can set rates based on the time it takes for you to complete tasks, which demonstrates how valuable your skills are. Effective use of time can also help you manage multiple projects, so you are able to accept work on a continuous basis.

Now that you understand how to set yourself up for success as a free-lancer, let's cross over to Part 7 and consider how you can manage to work a day job while building your online business.

PART SEVEN
WHAT'S NEXT?

CHAPTER 19
WAYS TO START YOUR OWN BUSINESS WHILE WORKING A FULL-TIME JOB

The secret of change is to focus all of your energy not on fighting the old, but on building the new.

SOCRATES

THE CHALLENGES AND OPPORTUNITIES OF STARTING A BUSINESS WHILE WORKING FULL-TIME

The thought of being a full-time employee and part-time entrepreneur may sound a bit over the top. Working for somebody else and being your own boss have always been seen as strictly opposing ideas. You may find yourself feeling pressured to choose one or the other, or delay starting your business because you aren't ready to say goodbye to your stable job.

However, you shouldn't have to pick between a traditional 9-to-5 and entrepreneurship because you can manage these commitments simultaneously. You may be asking yourself, "But how?" Well, it all boils down to having effective time management skills, creating a business model that complements your lifestyle, and automating as much of your business as you can.

Instead of wrecking your brain trying to think of how you are going to cope with the demands of your day job and business, focus on planning the kind of lifestyle that merges both responsibilities without any friction.

Below are just a few considerations to make when planning out your new life:

1. Start correctly and legally

Check your workplace policies and procedures to make sure that your business wouldn't be considered a "conflict of interest." If you are not sure, seek guidance from your company's HR or a business lawyer.

2. Do your research

Before you jump in with both feet, take the time to research the business you are getting into, the kinds of duties you will be in charge of, how much time and money it will require, and generally how long it takes before your business requires less of you. The last thing you want when you are managing a day job and business is unexpected problems that you didn't anticipate (worst of all if these problems need money to fix). Therefore, don't skip over the research stage, and if possible, speak to someone who has been in the industry for a while.

3. Live a lean lifestyle

Starting a business is like having a newborn baby. For the first few years, it will demand a lot of your attention and resources. Living a lean lifestyle helps you save cash, in case you need to attend to a business crisis. Of course, you shouldn't deprive yourself of creature comforts. But in the back of your mind, it is important to remember that you have a needy business that constantly requires investment.

4. Build a support system

Time won't always be on your side when you are working a day job and running a business. It can be comforting to be surrounded by people who are encouraging and understand the sacrifices you are making. Your support system doesn't need to consist of close friends and family only. It could also include colleagues, business partners, mentors, or online experts that you follow. Audit your support system regularly to make sure that the people nearest to you are building you up with their words and actions.

5. Remember to consult with your virtual assistant

ChatGPT was made for busy professionals who need access to reliable information, without spending hours looking for it. As someone who will be juggling two careers at the same time, ChatGPT can help you complete tasks for both jobs and streamline your processes.

IN SUMMARY

- You don't need to choose between keeping your day job and starting an online business. The truth is you can handle both without compromising your well-being. It simply takes doing the necessary research and planning what your new routine and lifestyle will require of you.
- Remember to seek support in the form of friends, family, and business acquaintances who can offer emotional support, share skills and knowledge, and help you through the transition period. There are also many tech tools available, such as ChatGPT that can take some of the workload off your shoulders.

Now that you know it is possible to juggle a corporate and business career, let's cross over to the final chapter and discuss the right time to focus on your business full-time.

CHAPTER 20

WHEN TO QUIT YOUR FULL-TIME JOB

If something is important enough, or you believe something is important enough, even if you are scared, you will keep going.

ELON MUSK

QUIZ: ARE YOU READY FOR AN ENTREPRENEURIAL LIFE?

Are you entertaining the thought of running your business full-time? If so, you need to first understand what entrepreneurship really entails. For a moment, put aside that idealized image of entrepreneurship that you often see on social media, and focus on the grind that is required to build a successful business. Consider the early mornings and late nights, the sacrifices to your lifestyle, and the potential setbacks. This is what building a startup looks like.

To test whether you are truly ready for an entrepreneurial life, take this short quiz before continuing with the chapter:

Instructions: Read the following questions and answer "Yes" or "No" when applicable.

Questions	Yes	No
1. Do you spend a lot of time daydreaming about being a full-time entrepreneur?		
2. Do you spend your free time brainstorming and researching information about your business?		
3. Do you feel like you have found your passion by pursuing your business venture?		
4. Are you a proactive problem-solver, someone who jumps at opportunities to address challenges?		
5. Do you have tested and effective stress management techniques to implement during difficult situations?		
6. Do you have a positive perspective on failure?		
7. Do you have a solid support network, consisting of people who can help you build a successful business?		
8. Do you have three to six months' worth of savings put aside?		
9. Have you proven that your business model is capable of generating income?		
10. Are you willing to accept the risk of running a business, knowing that success isn't guaranteed?		

If you have answered "Yes" to 7 or more questions, you have what it takes to run your business full-time!

REACHING THE CROSSROAD

Yes, it's true. You can juggle two careers at one time. In fact, this is even easier to manage when you are running an online or freelance business. However, there will come a stage when your business takes off and starts demanding more of your time. Or perhaps you have discovered new business opportunities that you would like to explore.

This is usually when you reach a crossroads and have to choose between staying at your day job and doing as much as you can to keep the business afloat, or quitting your day job and investing your full attention to making your business grow.

Quitting your day job sounds terrifying, but there are some benefits to it, such as the following:

- Quitting your job enables you to spend more time problem-solving and growing your business. When you do this, you are able to fail faster, refine your business model, and generate more revenue.
- Quitting your job can improve your mental health, which allows you to have a positive outlook on life, and spread that optimism in your business. You will also have more time to rest and achieve balance in your life.
- While there are no guarantees that your business will succeed, if it is profitable you can accumulate more money than you did working a full-time job. More money means greater freedom to live the lifestyle of your dreams!
- Quitting your job can boost your confidence and help you align your lifestyle with your core values. It can also be the gateway to pursuing projects that are meaningful and create a sense of purpose.

If these benefits sound enticing, read on to know the right time to quit your day job!

TIMING YOUR EXIT FROM YOUR DAY JOB

Here's the cold and harsh truth: About 90% of startup businesses fail; 10% of them fail within the first year and 51% fail within five years (Embroker, 2023).

The main reason why startups fail is misunderstanding market needs, but the second is running out of cash to fund the business. As a business owner, this data is enough to cause you to contemplate holding on to your stable job for just a while longer. However, your business doesn't need to be part of the statistics.

Timing is essential when planning your exit from your day job. For instance, if you quit your job too soon, while your business is still in the growth phase, it is possible to run out of funds. To reduce as much risk as possible, you should aim to quit your job when your business is able to sustain itself (i.e. generate enough income to pay off its expenses each month).

You might be wondering what that might look like in practical terms. Here are a few green flags that you are ready to quit your full-time job:

1. Your business generates enough income

The clearest sign that it is safe to quit your day job is when your business is making money. There is no fixed rule about how much money it should be making, but some experts recommend two-thirds of your salary. You can decide what your magic number is based on your earning expectations. How much you are comfortable making before you quit your day job may also be dependent on your monthly financial obligations.

2. You have built up an emergency fund

Startup businesses are incredibly risky because you are not guaranteed consistent income every month. Some months you might make a fortune and other months you break even. To ensure that you aren't negatively affected by the fluctuations of income, it is important to have an emergency savings account to dip into when you aren't able to make your monthly financial obligations. At a minimum, your emergency fund should have three to six months' worth of savings to cover unexpected personal and business expenses.

3. You have passed the testing phase of your business model

If you are still trying to figure out if your business has a market, keep your day job. The cost of trial and error is extremely expensive and can take up the majority of your startup capital. Only when you have tested and refined your business model can you start considering actively running the business full-time. Until then, continue to play around with your business concept, conducting research and finding your competitive advantage.

4. You have a solid five-year plan

Future planning is important when you are transitioning to being a full-time entrepreneur. To prevent your business from becoming stagnant, you need to envision where you want to be in a few years' time. Your vision will keep you focused and limit potential distractions. It can also help you cut costs, scale your business, or even seek funding when your business reaches that stage. Your plan can be as detailed as you would like.

For example, you can draft a five-year comprehensive business plan that includes strategies, budgets, and deadlines that will guide you through the first five years. Since a business plan is a living document, you can make adjustments to your plan whenever necessary.

5. You are ready to make the leap

The best time to quit your day job is when you are ready to. Signs of being ready could be tangible, such as making enough money from your business to sustain your livelihood. But sometimes, your readiness could be predicated on how you feel. On an intuitive level, you just know that it is the right time to make the career transition. The thought of being a full-time entrepreneur doesn't intimidate you anymore because you have developed confidence in your ability to succeed!

These green flags are guidelines for knowing when it is a good time to quit your job. Nevertheless, they don't guarantee that running your business will be smooth sailing. Entrepreneurship will always be a risky endeavor, but the potential returns make the risk worth it!

Don't forget to utilize ChatGPT during this stage of your career. For instance, you might need more information about your business model to see whether it is viable. Or you may need to draft the perfect resignation letter to send to your boss. Whatever your needs are, this handy virtual assistant is at your service!

IN SUMMARY

- It is possible to manage a day job and a business, but at some point, you will need to choose between the comfort of a paycheck or growing your business.
- The benefits of being a full-time entrepreneur include investing more time into growing your business, creating a better work-life balance, and achieving your wildest financial goals!
- Quitting your job is all about getting the timing right. Before you seriously consider transitioning to entrepreneurship, make sure that you have passed the testing phase, have proven that your business can make money, and have at least three to six months' worth of savings put aside.

HELP OTHERS SEE CHATGPT AS A POWERFUL TOOL FOR PROFESSIONAL SUCCESS...

A short review from you could make a world of difference to someone who feels like they have to stay in a job they are unhappy with, or earn a salary that simply isn't enough to pay the bills.

By giving your honest opinion of this book, you'll show other readers how ChatGPT can help them earn double what they're making now or more—whether they wish to be a freelancer or start their own business.

Scan the QR-code below to go directly to the review page.

Thank you for your support. My aim is to help readers see AI as a tool that can propel them to a financially stable life. And your words can inspire them to send ChatGPT their first money-making prompt!

CONCLUSION

To become financially independent, you must turn part of your income into capital; turn capital into enterprise; turn enterprise into profit; turn a profit into an investment, and turn the investment into financial independence.

JIM ROHN

One of the motivations for finding ways to make more money is to achieve financial independence. You might envision living life on your own terms and having the freedom to choose how to spend your time.

Making money isn't rocket science, but that doesn't mean it is easy either. There are quite a number of hoops you need to jump through before you secure multiple streams of income. Granted, before the invention of the internet, making money was a lot harder than it is now. If you weren't physically exerting energy, you wouldn't get very far.

Technological tools have democratized the playing field, allowing anybody with a stable internet connection to make money online. The best part is that you aren't required to sacrifice all of your time and energy since these tools are designed to handle manual and time-consuming tasks.

Excitement filled the air when ChatGPT was first released back in 2022. While a few were skeptical about what this would mean for their job security, the majority of people couldn't wait to assign a portion of their duties to the chatbot. The intelligence, relevance, and accuracy of ChatGPT make it the closest AI tool to an actual human being—even though it is still decades away from thinking like a real human.

Some of the perks ChatGPT is known for are enhancing productivity, extracting insights from data, and assisting with time management. For anyone who works a 9-to-5 job, using ChatGPT can increase the quality and efficiency of carrying out tasks, saving a lot of time in the process. However, this is not all the chatbot is good for. Aspiring and seasoned entrepreneurs have also found value in using ChatGPT to build and grow their businesses, which has lowered the barriers of starting businesses.

Throughout this book, you have been shown various ways to use Chat-GPT, whether it is for business or leisure. You have also been given examples of 40 skillful prompts to use when seeking to extract quality results from the chatbot. Based on your career goals and financial needs, you can decide whether freelancing or building an online business is the right business model for you. If you are still not certain, perhaps this is a decision ChatGPT can help you with?

But regardless of which model you end up choosing, it is a fact that the process of making money online has been simplified for you by AI tools like ChatGPT, enabling you to achieve financial independence!

If you are walking away from this book feeling more confident about making money online using ChatGPT, please show support by leaving a review.

GLOSSARY

Artificial intelligence: A technological system that is able to learn and interpret data to assist with problem-solving, research, or analyzing large amounts of information.

Chatbot: An AI tool that facilitates interactive conversations between the AI machine and human user.

ChatGPT: A chatbot designed using generative AI.

Content: Creative material produced for the purpose of enjoyment or marketing a business.

Content optimization: The process of making content "discoverable" on search engines like Google, by incorporating frequently searched keywords into the material.

Freelance business: A type of online business started by a freelancer, in which they are both the employer and the employee providing a service.

Freelancer: A self-employed individual who seeks ongoing contractual work by marketing their skills online.

Generative AI: A type of artificial intelligence system that is designed to assist with content creation, such as producing text, image, audio, and video material.

Online business: A type of business that exists online and conducts business activities through digital channels.

OpenAI: A research-based company that seeks to investigate and develop artificial intelligence tools.

Prompt: A question or instruction that is given to ChatGPT to initiate a conversation.

Prompt engineering: The process of crafting skillful prompts that are capable of extracting insights from data and high-quality results.

Virtual assistant: A digital assistant who could be a human working remotely or a tool built by AI, which is designed to support individuals and businesses in completing administrative tasks.

REFERENCES

A Better LemonadeStand. (2020, July 14). How to make a business plan for an online business. A Better Lemonade Stand. https://www.abetterlemonadestand.com/online-business-plan/

Admin. (2022, December 21). The best ChatGPT quotes. Supply Chain Today. https://www.supplychaintoday.com/best-chatgpt-quotes/

Arford, K. (2023, April 3). How to build a stand-out online presence (+why it's so important). LocaliQ. https://localiq.com/blog/online-presence/

Athow, D. (2023, March 2). Best freelance websites in 2021. TechRadar. https://www.techradar.com/best/best-freelance-websites

Baker, K. (2023, June 23). The ultimate guide to content marketing in 2020. HubSpot. https://blog.hubspot.com/marketing/content-marketing

Bensinger, G. (2023, February 21). ChatGPT launches boom in AI-written e-books on Amazon. Reuters. https://www.reuters.com/technology/chatgpt-launches-boom-ai-written-e-books-amazon-2023-02-21/

Berra, Y. (n.d.). Top 25 business plan quotes (of 106). A-Z Quotes. https://www.azquotes.com/quotes/topics/business-plan.html

Berry, T. (2010, June 15). Why plan your business? Look at this data. Tim Berry BPlans. https://timberry.bplans.com/real-data-on-the-success-of-business-planning/

Bertrand, G. (2016, February 2). "Without data you're just another person with an opinion." LinkedIn. https://www.linkedin.com/pulse/without-data-youre-just-another-person-opinion-gaelle-bertrand/

Blue Corona. (2016, March 24). 50 Digital marketing quotes. Blue Corona. https://www.bluecorona.com/blog/50-inspirational-marketing-quotes/

Boitnott, J. (2015, July 28). 25 Quotes about making money and keeping perspective. Entrepreneur. https://www.entrepreneur.com/money-finance/25-quotes-about-making-money-and-keeping-perspective/248759

Bosze, A. (n.d.). Business plan for online shops: how to create it from scratch. Doofinder. https://www.doofinder.com/en/blog/e-commerce-business-plan

Bouchard, L. (2022, December 12). Prompting explained: How to talk to ChatGPT. Louis Bouchard. https://www.louisbouchard.ai/prompting-explained/

Buckland, T. (2018, January 5). 9 Tips for starting your online business while working full time. Classy Career Girl. https://www.classycareergirl.com/online-business-working-full-time-start/

Campbell, K. (2023, June 8). 2019 Online reputation management statistics [May update]. ReputationX. https://blog.reputationx.com/online-reputation-management-statistics

Can you really handle the entrepreneurial life? Check these 5 signs. (2014, August 4).

Entrepreneur.   https://www.entrepreneur.com/starting-a-business/can-you-really-handle-the-entrepreneurial-life-check-these/235919

Casazza, N. (2019, September 23). Five core productivity principles. Nahid Coaching and Mentoring. https://www.coachnahid.com/five-core-productivity-principles/

ChatGPT quotes (30 quotes). (n.d.). Goodreads. https://www.goodreads.com/quotes/tag/chatgpt#:

Chu, M. (2017, April 24). Why you should work your day job while starting a business. Inc Africa.   https://incafrica.com/library/melissa-chu-why-you-should-work-your-day-job-while-starting-a-business

Chui, M., Roberts, R., & Yee, L. (2022, December 20). How generative AI could change your business. Www.mckinsey.com. https://www.mckinsey.com/capabilities/quantum black/our-insights/generative-ai-is-here-how-tools-like-chatgpt-could-change-your-business

Coursera. (2023, May 17). ChatGPT 101: What is generative AI (and how to use it). Coursera. https://www.coursera.org/articles/chatgpt

Das, T. (2021, July 10). 10 Tips you can use to get more clients as a freelancer. MUO. https://www.makeuseof.com/tips-use-get-more-clients-freelancer/

del Principe, C. (2022, July 26). Online customer service: 16 Data-backed ways to improve it. Hubspot. https://blog.hubspot.com/service/online-customer-service

Derungs, A. (2023, January 30). How to make money with ChatGPT: 13 Ways to profit in 2023! Niche Pursuits. https://www.nichepursuits.com/how-to-make-money-with-chatgpt/

DevriX. (2022, July 21). User attention span: the biggest challenge for marketers [2022]. DevriX. https://devrix.com/tutorial/user-attention-span-2022/

Diaz, M. (2023, April 13). How to use ChatGPT: Everything you need to know. ZDNET. https://www.zdnet.com/article/how-to-use-chatgpt/

Djuraskovic, O. (2021, January 18). 40 Freelance stats and trends 2023 (pandemic effects on the industry). FirstSiteGuide. https://firstsiteguide.com/freelance-stats/#:

Dunne, C. (2018, December 27). 40 Motivational quotes for work productivity and success. Tameday. https://www.tameday.com/motivational-quotes-for-work-productivity/

Embroker. (2020, June 19). 106 Must-know startup statistics for 2020. Embroker. https://www.embroker.com/blog/startup-statistics/

Entrepreneur Staff. (2023, February 16). ChatGPT: What is it and how does it work? Entrepreneur. https://www.entrepreneur.com/science-technology/chatgpt-what-is-it-and-how-does-it-work/445014

Farese, D. (2019, March 29). How to do market research: A 6-step guide. HubSpot. https://blog.hubspot.com/marketing/market-research-buyers-journey-guide

Fell, J. (2022, October 12). 7 Benefits of starting an online business. Entrepreneur Guide. https://www.entrepreneur.com/guide/side-hustles/7-benefits-of-starting-an-online-business

Finance Quick Fix. (2022, November 25). Great reasons to make money online. Finance Quick Fix. https://financequickfix.com/great-reasons-to-make-money-online/

Flaneur Life. (2022, July 15). 46 Galvanizing quotes about online business success. Flaneur Life. https://www.flaneurlife.com/quotes-about-online-business/

Flynn, J. (2023, February 19). 20 Incredible online business statistics [2022]. Zippia. https://www.zippia.com/advice/online-business-statistics/

Fresh Business Thinking. (2016, August 2). Quarter of businesses don't do any market research. Fresh Business Thinking. https://www.freshbusinessthinking.com/purpose/quarter-of-businesses-dont-do-any-market-research/42919.article#:

GT Correspondent. (2023, March 23). Can ChatGPT replace Google? Here is how ChatGPT works. TimesNow. https://www.timesnownews.com/technology-science/can-chat gpt-replace-google-here-is-how-chatgpt-works-article-98942256#:

Halder, S. (2023, March 8). Researching potential niches to target using ChatGPT. Medium. https://zealousi.medium.com/researching-potential-niches-to-target-using-chatgpt-d0415be2e49b?_branch_match_id

Hardy, B. (2018, July 20). *How To Become More Intelligent (According to Einstein)*. https://medium.com/the-mission/if-youre-not-changing-as-a-person-then-you-re-not-intelli gent-according-to-einstein-73ba950d99d5

Hippler, K. (2020, May 3). From freelancer to agency: Is it the right move for you? Upwork. https://www.upwork.com/resources/from-freelancer-to-agency

Howell, J. (2023, April 20). The importance of prompt engineering in the AI revolution. 101 Blockchains. https://101blockchains.com/importance-of-ai-prompt-engineering/

Huntlancer Team. (2021). 50 Motivational quotes for freelancers and entrepreneurs. Huntlancer. https://www.huntlancer.com/motivational-quotes-for-freelancers-and-entrepreneurs/

Insights Editor. (2022, July 6). "The secret of change is to focus all of your energy, not on fighting the old, but on building the new"- Socrates. (10M). InsightsIAS. https://www.insightsonindia.com/2022/07/06/the-secret-of-change-is-to-focus-all-of-your-energy-not-on-fighting-the-old-but-on-building-the-new-socrates-10m/

Keyes, B. (2023, January 26). 20 Amazing ChatGPT prompts: 10x your productivity today. Medium. https://medium.com/@productivitybee/20-amazing-chatgpt-prompts-10x-your-productivity-today-3b306e455dc5

Kitzmiller, H. (2022, December 20). 9 Online business models for 2023 (Types of online businesses). Vital Dollar. https://vitaldollar.com/online-business-models/

Klingenberg, A. (n.d.). Arne Klingenberg quote. Goodreads. https://www.goodreads.com/author/show/775530.Arne_Klingenberg

Kopp, C. M. (2023, March 25). Understanding business models. Investopedia. https://www.investopedia.com/terms/b/businessmodel.asp

Kumar, N. (2023, January 28). eLearning trends: Top 8 L&D trends to watch out for in 2023. ELearning Industry. https://elearningindustry.com/elearning-trends-top-ld-trends-to-watch-out-for-in-2023

Kumar, S. S. (2021, September 24). Top 10 requirements of starting an online business. Marketplace Startup Articles . https://www.rentallscript.com/resources/require ments-to-start-an-online-business/

L, D. (2023, March 7). Rise of robots - Jobs lost to automation statistics in 2023. Leftronic. https://leftronic.com/blog/jobs-lost-to-automation-statistics/#:

LoCascio, R. (2023, April 2). I tried using ChatGPT to write this article. Fast Company. https://www.fastcompany.com/90844120/i-tried-using-chatgpt-to-write-this-article

Luke, R. (2021, June 13). 61 Financial freedom quotes and steps to achieve it. Yahoo Finance. https://finance.yahoo.com/news/61-financial-freedom-quotes-steps-040400309.html

March, L. (2023, January 31). Online market research: What it is and how to do it. Similarweb Blog. https://www.similarweb.com/blog/research/market-research/online-market-research/

Marinaki, A. (2023, May 31). 80 Glorious marketing quotes to empower and inspire you. Moosend. https://moosend.com/blog/marketing-quotes/

McCormick, K. (2023, April 13). The 25 best ways to increase your online presence in 2021 (+free tools). Wordstream. https://www.wordstream.com/blog/ws/2021/05/17/increase-online-presence

Mileva, G. (2023, May 24). The ultimate AI prompt optimization guide for 2023. Influencer Marketing Hub. https://influencermarketinghub.com/ai-prompt-optimization/

Miszczak, P. (2023, February 25). Prompt engineering: The ultimate guide 2023 [GPT-3 & ChatGPT]. Businessolution. https://businessolution.org/prompt-engineering/

Mottesi, C. (2023, February 8). 6 Uses of ChatGPT for customer service. Invgate. https://blog.invgate.com/chatgpt-for-customer-service

Mottola, M. (2023, March 30). How ChatGPT and generative AI can impact the freelance economy. Forbes. https://www.forbes.com/sites/matthewmottola/2023/03/30/how-chatgpt-and-generative-ai-can-impact-the-freelance-economy/?sh=225bd5e3fac6

Natasha. (2023, June 15). 100 Ways to use ChatGPT-4 to increase your productivity. AI Vanguard. https://medium.com/ai-vanguard/100-ways-to-use-chatgpt-to-increase-your-productivity-e38c4a1c4740

Nield, D. (2023, February 24). 6 Ways ChatGPT is actually useful right now. Popular Science. https://www.popsci.com/diy/chatgpt-use-cases/

Nielsen, J. (2023, April 2). ChatGPT lifts business professionals' productivity and improves work quality. Nielsen Norman Group. https://www.nngroup.com/articles/chatgpt-productivity/

Norton, R. (n.d.). Richie Norton quote. Goodreads. https://www.goodreads.com/author/show/5821896.Richie_Norton

Nucleus AI. (2023, April 2). ChatGPT takes the helm as CEO, turns startup profitable in a week, and forecasts €400,000 annual profit. Your Story. https://yourstory.com/2023/04/chatgpt-ai-ceo-profitable-startup-aisthetic-apparel?utm_pageloadtype=scroll

OpenAI. (2023a, July 3). ChatGPT (July 03 version) [A true friend... Example: Gossips behind your back - False Example: Offers emotional support - True Example: Does not apologize after offending you - False Example: Respects your boundaries - True Classify this statement: Downplays your success]. OpenAI. https://chat.openai.com/?model=text-davinci-002-render-sha

OpenAI. (2023b, July 3). ChatGPT (July 03 version) [As a startup print-on-demand business, who would be my two biggest competitors? Identify the strengths and weaknesses of each competitor. Your response should be less than 200 words.]. OpenAI. https://chat.openai.com/?model=text-davinci-002-render-sha

OpenAI. (2023c, July 3). ChatGPT (July 03 version) [Based on the outline provided, complete a draft of the executive summary, using only 100 words. Mention that the business was started by Katie and her husband Steve in their basement studio.]. OpenAI. https://chat.openai.com/?model=text-davinci-002-render-sha

OpenAI. (2023d, July 3). ChatGPT (July 03 version) [Based on the preferences of suburban mothers between the ages of 40 and 60 who are planning for retirement, what are the best media forms to share content? Provide a list with examples of type of content.]. OpenAI. https://chat.openai.com/?model=text-davinci-002-render-sha

OpenAI. (2023e, July 3). ChatGPT (July 03 version) [Based on the topic of purchasing logo designs online, list the 10 most frequently asked questions by college students.]. OpenAI. https://chat.openai.com/?model=text-davinci-002-render-sha

OpenAI. (2023f, July 3). ChatGPT (July 03 version) [Be honest ChatGPT, will you replace my job as a freelance writer one day?]. OpenAI. https://chat.openai.com/?model=text-davinci-002-render-sha

OpenAI. (2023g, July 3). ChatGPT (July 03 version) [Create a detailed audience persona for the target audience mentioned above. Include key information, such as audience likes and dislikes, and common challenges faced related to print-on-demand businesses.]. OpenAI. https://chat.openai.com/?model=text-davinci-002-render-sha

OpenAI. (2023h, July 3). ChatGPT (July 03 version) [Create a list of one quality, with five sample phrases, to inform my brand voice. We are an online coaching business offering individual and group mentorship services. Keep descriptions short.]. OpenAI. https://chat.openai.com/?model=text-davinci-002-render-sha

OpenAI. (2023i, July 3). ChatGPT (July 03 version) [Create a schedule for a typical productive morning (without descriptions).]. OpenAI. https://chat.openai.com/

OpenAI. (2023j, July 3). ChatGPT (July 03 version) [Create a two minute, daily workout routine that can help me lose 5 kgs (2 pounds) per month. Example: 10 reps sit ups. Keep descriptions short.]. OpenAI. https://chat.openai.com/?model=text-davinci-002-render-sha

OpenAI. (2023k, July 3). ChatGPT (July 03 version) [Create an email script, using only 100 words, to request a review from customers, after they have received their product from us. Include details on how they can leave the review. For example, follow the link to our website.]. OpenAI. https://chat.openai.com/?model=text-davinci-002-render-sha

OpenAI. (2023l, July 3). ChatGPT (July 03 version) [Here are the top 5 most popular long-tail keywords for logo design trends:]. OpenAI. https://chat.openai.com/?model=text-davinci-002-render-sha

OpenAI. (2023m, July 3). ChatGPT (July 03 version) [Here is my customer's problem: Customer is trying to add items in her shopping cart but the items won't reflect. Shopping cart is empty despite her attempts. Please help me solve the problem by offering three possible solutions.]. OpenAI. https://chat.openai.com/?model=text-davinci-002-render-sha

OpenAI. (2023n, July 3). ChatGPT (July 03 version) [I am starting a podcasting business. Please provide an outline, without descriptions, for my business plan.]. OpenAI. https://chat.openai.com/?model=text-davinci-002-render-sha

OpenAI. (2023o, July 3). ChatGPT (July 03 version) [I am starting a print-on-demand business. Please help me identify a target audience. For example, identify the demographics of people who would be interested in my business. Give an explanation why they are the right audience.]. OpenAI. https://chat.openai.com/?model=text-davinci-002-render-sha

OpenAI. (2023p, July 3). ChatGPT (July 03 version) [I am using email marketing to connect with suburban mothers between the ages of 40 and 60. List content goals to focus on.]. OpenAI. https://chat.openai.com/?model=text-davinci-002-render-sha

OpenAI. (2023q, July 3). ChatGPT (July 03 version) [I have $500. What is the best business model for me?]. OpenAI. https://chat.openai.com/c/06d71dea-432b-4aac-ab2d-60914956aae0

OpenAI. (2023r, July 3). ChatGPT (July 03 version) [I want to start a business selling print-on-demand t-shirts online. Please provide me with the core data on the industry, keep it very short]. OpenAI. https://chat.openai.com/?model=text-davinci-002-render-sha

OpenAI. (2023s, July 3). ChatGPT (July 03 version) [Identify two of the best online business models for writing services.]. OpenAI. https://chat.openai.com/

OpenAI. (2023t, July 3). ChatGPT (July 03 version) [List 10 long-tail keywords, for the topic of logo designs, most commonly searched by college students.]. OpenAI. https://chat.openai.com/?model=text-davinci-002-render-sha

OpenAI. (2023u, July 3). ChatGPT (July 03 version) [List without providing a description, the top 5 most popular keywords for logo design trends.]. OpenAI. https://chat.openai.com/?model=text-davinci-002-render-sha

OpenAI. (2023v, July 3). ChatGPT (July 03 version) [My customer left the following review online: "I am underwhelmed about my recent experience working with Sam. I asked her to write a few SEO articles for my blog. While she is pleasant to work with, I find her time management questionable." Provide a 50 word empathetic script.]. OpenAI. https://chat.openai.com/?model=text-davinci-002-render-sha

OpenAI. (2023w, July 3). ChatGPT (July 03 version) [What are 5 most popular sub-topics related to buying logos online?]. OpenAI. https://chat.openai.com/?model=text-davinci-002-render-sha

OpenAI. (2023x, July 3). ChatGPT (July 03 version) [What are 5 most popular sub-topics, without description, related to logo design services?]. OpenAI. https://chat.openai.com/?model=text-davinci-002-render-sha

OpenAI. (2023y, July 3). ChatGPT (July 03 version) [Which digital channels are the best for connecting with suburban mothers between the ages of 40 and 60, who are planning for retirement? Rank them, without providing a description.]. OpenAI. https://chat.openai.com/?model=text-davinci-002-render-sha

OpenAI. (2023z, July 3). ChatGPT (July 03 version) [Write a social media announcement, using only 200 characters, about a 15% discount on graphic design services over Thanksgiving weekend. Make the announcement relevant to the Instagram audience.]. OpenAI. https://chat.openai.com/?model=text-davinci-002-render-sha

Overall Motivation. (2021, November 4). 65 Niche quotes on success in life. Overall Motivation. https://www.overallmotivation.com/quotes/niche-quotes/

Pande, K. (2018). 47 Uplifting entrepreneur quotes to ignite your drive. Hubspot. https://blog.hubspot.com/sales/motivational-quotes-from-some-of-the-world-most-successful-entrepreneurs

Patwa, A. (2023, April 18). 20 Proven ways to make money with ChatGPT with examples. Earning a Bit. https://earningabit.com/make-money-with-chatgpt/

Pinegar, G. (2020, February 3). How to get freelance clients (7 ideas that work in 2021). Millo. https://millo.co/how-to-get-freelance-clients

Radnai, G. (2023, May 24). 250+ Resume statistics: Length, success rates, and more. MarketSplash. https://marketsplash.com/resume-statistics/

Renaissance Rachel. (2023, March 31). Prompting: Getting AI models to do what you want. Renaissance Rachel. https://renaissancerachel.com/prompting/

Ryan, E. (2022, June 7). How to do market research for your online business in 2023. Website Builder Expert. https://www.websitebuilderexpert.com/building-online-stores/market-research-for-online-business/

Sachdeva, A. (2023, February 23). How to use ChatGPT for market research. GapScout. https://gapscout.com/blog/how-to-use-chatgpt-for-market-research/

Selfgood Team. (2022, December 14). How to land high-paying gigs by negotiating freelancer rates. Selfgood. https://selfgood.com/blog/negotiating-freelancer-rates

Shakil, D. (2023, January 8). 13 Best AI businesses to start with ChatGPT (Jan 2023). Online Biz Assets. https://onlinebizassets.com/chatgpt-business-ideas/

Simpson, A. (2023, March 2). 9 ChatGPT success stories to highlight what you can do in 2023. Niche Pursuits. https://www.nichepursuits.com/chatgpt-success-stories/

Sivakumar, B. (2023, April 25). What is freelancing? How to become a freelancer? Feedough. https://www.feedough.com/what-is-freelancing-how-to-become-a-freelancer-the-actionable-guide/

Smith, H. V. (n.d.). Self discipline quotes (214 quotes). Goodreads. https://www.goodreads.com/quotes/tag/self-discipline?page=2

Smullen, D. (2023, April 19). How to use ChatGPT for keyword research. Search Engine Journal. https://www.searchenginejournal.com/chatgpt-for-keyword-research/483848/

Šobak, P. (2023, April 19). How to start your own freelance business in 8 simple steps. Better Proposals Blog. https://betterproposals.io/blog/start-freelance-business/

Statista. (2023, January). Knowledge of generative AI in social media US 2023. Statista. https://www.statista.com/statistics/1368831/familiarity-with-social-media-in-the-united-states/

Stemann, P. (2022, October 19). 17 Tips to manage your freelance projects. Planzer. https://planzer.io/17-tips-to-manage-your-freelance-projects/

Sumrak, J. (2023, March 1). When to quit your job and go all-in on your side hustle. Foundr. https://foundr.com/articles/building-a-business/when-to-quit-your-job

Sylva. (2017, November 23). 15 Inspirational quotes from leaders in tech. Page Freezer. https://blog.pagefreezer.com/15-inspirational-quotes-from-leaders-in-tech

Team Building. (2021, December 14). 66 Best customer service quotes for work in 2022. Team Building. https://teambuilding.com/blog/customer-service-quotes

Teja, R. (2023, February 14). 25 Things you can do with ChatGPT. TechWiser. https://techwiser.com/things-you-can-do-with-chatgpt/#5-Make-Conversations-About-Your-Favorite-Topic

Thrasyvoulou, S. (2023, March 21). Why AI can't replace freelancers and other human jobs. TalentDesk. https://www.talentdesk.io/blog/why-ai-cant-replace-freelancers

Timothy, M. (2022, October 28). How to negotiate a higher freelance rate: 7 tips. MUO. https://www.makeuseof.com/negotiate-higher-freelance-pay/

Upwork Team. (2022, April 6). What is freelancing? Basics and popular jobs. Upwork. https://www.upwork.com/resources/what-is-freelancing#benefits

Vega, M. (2019, November 13). 17+ Jobs lost to automation statistics in 2020 [updated]. TechJury. https://techjury.net/blog/jobs-lost-to-automation-statistics/

Victor, A. (2023, February 27). Top 17 industry applications of ChatGPT. Daffodil. https://insights.daffodilsw.com/blog/top-17-industry-applications-of-chatgpt

Wolinski, P. (2023, January 19). How to use ChatGPT: Step-by-step instructions. Tom's Guide. https://www.tomsguide.com/how-to/how-to-use-chatgpt

Woodward, M. (2023a, June 12). *Fiverr users statistics: How many people use Fiverr in 2023.* SearchLogistics. https://www.searchlogistics.com/learn/statistics/fiverr-users/#:~:text=Fiverr%20has%20almost%20become%20a

Woodward, M. (2023, June 12). Infographic statistics: How effective are infographics today? Search Logistics. https://www.searchlogistics.com/learn/statistics/infographic-statistics/#:

Zinkula, J., & Mok, A. (2023, March 21). A guy is using ChatGPT to turn $100 into a business making "as much money as possible." Here are the first 4 steps the AI chatbot gave him. Business Insider. https://www.businessinsider.com/how-to-use-chatgpt-to-start-business-make-money-quickly-2023-3